PREACHING IN
BLACK
&
WHITE

The great thing about *Preaching in Black and White* is that Drs. Wiersbe and Bailey actually listen to each other as well as mutually instruct. Here is essential wisdom for those who would presume to preach midst the swirling cultures of the twenty-first century.

— R. Kent Hughes, pastor, College Church in Wheaton

A landmark book for believers on the biblical concept of the unity of the body of Christ. Two world-class preachers interact on the dilemma of ethnic differences with helpful insights for every thinking communicator. Ignore this book at your own loss.

— Howard G. Hendricks, distinguished professor and chairman, Center for Christian Leadership, Dallas Theological Seminary

White or black, preacher or not, if you want to overcome racial distrust and disunity in the church, you need to read this book. It is a completely honest conversation between two men who trust each other enough and have experienced enough of each other's culture that they have extremely helpful things to say about getting along, working together, and learning from each other. If you are a preacher who wants to learn from some gifted, experienced, wise men whose preaching transcends culture, you need to read this book. It will likely be the best preaching book of the year. For the preacher who wants to grow—period—this is a must-read.

— Craig Brian Larson, editor of *Preaching Today Audio* and Preaching Today.com

This is the nuts and bolts of homiletics—two great preachers in dialogue about preaching. The more you read, the more you will be convinced that black and white are only the color of the preachers; the color of great preaching is always gold. Wiersbe and Bailey stand at the summit of such an Everest to remind us that the peaceable kingdom of honest homiletics is color blind.

— Calvin Miller, Beeson Divinity School

Preaching in Black and White ought to be read! Anything by Bailey and Wiersbe ought to be cherished.

— D. Stuart Briscoe, minister at large, Elmbrook Church

As a child in the heart of Central Africa, I learned to preach in "black and white." My father was an old-time missionary who lived among the nationals and mastered their language. Since then, I have sought to integrate black and white in every aspect of my ministry. I know that black and white keys on the piano produce the music of heaven that shaped the art and stirred the heart of great preaching! I thank God for this fine endeavor of Bailey and Wiersbe to harmonize what the devil would seek to ostracize.

— Dr. Stephen F. Olford, founder of the Stephen Olford Center for Biblical Preaching, Memphis, Tenn.

PREACHING IN
BLACK
&
WHITE

WHAT WE CAN LEARN
FROM EACH OTHER

E.K. BAILEY

WARREN W. WIERSBE

ZONDERVAN™

GRAND RAPIDS, MICHIGAN 49530 USA

Preaching in Black and White
Copyright © 2003 by E. K. Bailey and Warren W. Wiersbe

Requests for information should be addressed to:
Zondervan, *Grand Rapids, Michigan 49530*

Library of Congress Cataloging-in-Publication Data

Bailey, E. K., 1945–
    Preaching in black and white : what we can learn from each other / E. K. Bailey and
    Warren W. Wiersbe.
      p. cm.
    ISBN 0-310-24099-9
    1. Preaching. I. Wiersbe, Warren W. II. Title.
BV4211.3 .B35 2003
251'.00973 — dc21
                                        2002151183

Interior design by Tracey Moran

Printed in the United States of America

02 03 04 05 06 07 08 09 /❖ DC/ 10 9 8 7 6 5 4 3 2 1

CONTENTS

PART 1

WE TALK TOGETHER

CHAPTER 1

THE DYNAMICS
OF OUR HERITAGE

*B*lack preachers and white preachers have tended to minister in isolation within their separate communities, unaware of what they might learn from each other as members of the same body of Christ. Sometimes tensions and unfounded suspicions have festered between the communities. Yet as America has become increasingly diverse, church leaders and pastors need to become more sensitive to the needs of people from other cultural backgrounds in order to be able to lead the church effectively in a new century. This book serves as a groundbreaking attempt to bring together a noted black preacher and a noted white preacher to interact on the dynamics of pulpit ministry and what we can learn from each other's traditions and differing perspectives. Some surprises await us along the way.

You are invited to pull up a chair and listen in on a conversation that takes place in a comfortable lounge outside the office of Dr. E. K Bailey at Concord Missionary Baptist Church in Dallas, Texas. Across the table from Dr. Bailey sits the well-known pastor, conference preacher, and author Dr. Warren W. Wiersbe. These men became friends some years ago and enjoy exchanging humorous, friendly gibes across the table as they sip from steaming cups of coffee. They clearly enjoy each other's company. Although it's a weekday morning, the building bustles with activity in the adjoining offices, hallways, bookstore, and meeting rooms. Yet it becomes apparent that the heart of this active and growing church's ministry resides in its pulpit. You will sense this as we listen in on this extended conversation on a wide range of topics. At one point, we'll hear Dr. Bailey describe a beating he received

9

*from the police in California after having a double-barreled shotgun aimed
at his stomach. It is no wonder that this had an impact on his attitude
toward whites. Yet God's grace clearly worked to bring about some unexpected changes in his perspective on race. We'll also hear the story of when
E. K. forgot the second point in his sermon and how this brought the house
down with laughter.*

*The discussion with these two noted preachers begins with some ques-
tions about the background factors that have led to the differing approaches
to preaching in black and white churches. What historical influences have
shaped the black pulpit? Let's listen in.*

Historical Influences Shaping the Black Pulpit

Bailey: One of the most important historical influences on the black
pulpit is rooted in the way African-Americans were brought
to this country. It began with the experience of slavery—
leaving the west coast of Africa, coming through the middle
passage, and arriving in America in 1620. African-Americans were brought to this country for the sake of economic
gain through slavery; following slavery was Jim Crowism
and then following Jim Crowism was the civil rights movement. All of these experiences represent only different parts
of the same story. Biblically, the greatest influence would be
the Exodus of the Jewish people from Egypt. Slavery and
the Exodus have shaped reality for the African-American
community. Both of these factors form the most significant
underpinning of both the theological and the sociological
elements of black preaching, and even of some of the tech-
nical factors relating to the black pulpit today.

This does not mean that all African-American preachers
are wholehearted advocates of liberation theology. These
are just the fundamental influences on African-American
preaching. Liberation theology is correct in asserting that
the disenfranchised and the downtrodden should experience justice, economic empowerment, and positive social
mobilization. Further, the Bible specifically and explicitly
declares that God decries social and economic injustices.
However, the message of the gospel becomes muddled
when biblical salvation is deemed to occur when African-
Americans experience economic and social justice. Biblical

salvation properly understood is belief in the person and work of the Lord Jesus Christ demonstrated through faith in him. For Jesus Christ the Son of God died for our sins and was raised from the dead and is now seated in glory at the right hand of the Father.

Wiersbe: Is this only a subliminal influence, or is it something self-conscious that people are aware of today?

Bailey: It's glaring history. Your subconscious can't avoid it.

Wiersbe: You're born with it?

Bailey: Yes, it is inherited, and it certainly is experiential, no question about that. I think it's both subliminal and actual. It's passed down from one generation to the next, because most African-Americans feel that each generation has to fight the same battle over and over again. For that reason, it is passed down from one generation of leaders and preachers to the next, because they all address the same issues. From generation to generation the "enemy" changes its appearance and its position, but it does not change its basic essence. Therefore, every generation has to speak to the issue. Many people just can't seem to escape these generational matters.

Wiersbe: Does any generation ever grow out of it?

Bailey: Previous generations and mine had to grow through it, but the jury is still out on whether subsequent generations will grow out of it. Attitudes must continue to change, because it hasn't reached the point where it's no longer necessary to face this issue.

Wiersbe: Would, for example, an upper-middle-class black family think this way?

Bailey: Some would think this way. A few years ago *Time* magazine featured an article called "Taking Off the Mask." It revealed that upper-class African-Americans in corporate America were discovering more and more institutional racism than ever before. These problems haven't fully been solved yet in America. Though a black American has pursued the American dream and acquired an education, these trappings still don't guarantee first-class citizenship. In fact, many African-Americans feel isolated and very intimidated when they have been catapulted into a lofty position of being the only minority person in certain corporate settings. This makes them feel very isolated, mainly because they really don't have the camaraderie with their professional peers. Consequently, they're in a hurry to get back home to their community and especially home to their church.

When I initially began to open up our congregation here in Dallas, insisting that we had to model what the Bible says the church should look like, some of our corporate African-Americans complained. They said that their church was the only haven they had from white America. Now whites were going to come into our church! It was as if worshiping at their own church each week was their only time of reprieve, the one time when they knew they were safe. We don't feel safe the rest of the week, but we do feel safe at church. And now their pastor was going to eliminate that safe haven by allowing non-African-Americans to come into the church.

Jewish and Black Parallels

Wiersbe: It seems to me that when the African-American thinks of slavery, he thinks of a challenge. He says, "We're moving on. Let's go forward. We will overcome." The Jewish friends that I have think of the Holocaust and go into mourning. We can understand their feelings, but why the difference?

Bailey: I suppose part of it has to do with what really happened to each people group. African-Americans in this country suffered as slaves but weren't executed by the millions. There was no holocaust here in America. Also, some of the difference may be in the cultural values that each ethnic group passed down to its children.

Wiersbe: But our Jewish friends also go back to the Exodus, and you would think it would pull them together. Perhaps it has, but the emphasis has been on tribulation rather than liberation.

The Impact of the Civil Rights Movement

Slavery, obviously, is a very strong influence. What about the civil rights movement? Has that had an impact on black preaching, and if so, how?

Bailey: The civil rights movement was a key element of the total experience. It was significant due to an emphasis on a biblical "liberation theology" moving in. When the civil rights movement began, it gave my people hope. Their goal was now visible and thought to be attainable. Prior to that, we had dreamed about it but didn't really know whether or not it would come to fruition. The civil rights movement showed us the light at the end of the tunnel; now that we are closer, and if we press on, we can do much to reach the goal. It was a time for us to do something for ourselves. During the civil rights movement there was a positive emphasis on helping African-Americans shift their thinking from just hoping or watching to actually doing some things for themselves. The dominant culture we lived in, what was called "the system," was looked upon as Pharaoh in the Old Testament account of history. Pharaoh wasn't in the habit of setting slaves free, nor was the system. So if you're going to be free, you have to do some things to free yourself.

This meant we had to develop a theology of freedom. You will feel hard pressed to arrive at freedom without having a theology of freedom. The theology of freedom trickles down into a sociology of freedom, and that subsequently rolls down into an economics of freedom. So the civil rights movement now has moved to the "silver rights" movement. Now the baton has been handed to the next generation, because these developments are layered and tied to one another. Remember, you don't really have freedom as a citizen unless you also have economic freedom.

Does this explain why so many civil rights leaders were ministers?

Bailey: There were many dedicated laypeople involved in the civil rights movement. Most of the leaders were preachers who certainly understood the Exodus emphasis in the Bible. The civil rights movement led by Dr. Martin Luther King Jr.

receives much of the credit now, yet there were many facets to the civil rights movement that we must not overlook. The legal facet gave our country its first black Supreme Court justice, Thurgood Marshall, who also served as chief counsel for the NAACP from 1938–1950. Certain changes had to be carried out step by step through the courts. Then there were many student sit-ins, and certain issues were addressed through marches, often led by Dr. King. Marches were necessary to bring public pressure on local and national leaders and to challenge the moral integrity of our nation. We focused on the constitutional rights and expectations of all citizens. One of the reasons Dr. King gets so much credit is that he built on the foundation of the Constitution and the Bill of Rights and pricked our consciousness that America is built on guaranteed freedoms. The assumption by some white Americans that African-Americans were only one-fifth human was obviously a painfully gross misconception, and Dr. King addressed the issues invoking the law of nature and of nature's God, that all are equal, "endowed by their Creator with certain unalienable rights, that among these are life, liberty, and the pursuit of happiness."

It's not surprising that the civil rights movement was attacked in many ways. However, it must be said that there were miniscule pockets of support from the white community. The political, economic, and social institutions, along with the entertainment industry, attacked it. At that time in history the African-American preachers were in the forefront, because the church was the only instrument African-Americans had for united action and motivation. The church took on the central place. It's not much different now in the twenty-first century. The African-American church was and is the core and nucleus of our African-American community. Everything that we had—whether it was our social activities, our religious functions, or our entertainment—was all centered in the church. There was nothing more unifying or important in the civil rights movement than the local church and the churches working together. This, of course, determined the important place of leadership for the African-American preacher and pastor.

Did black preaching change as a result of the civil rights movement?

Bailey: I do believe preaching changed. Prior to the civil rights movement, when we were exiting slavery and entering Jim Crowism, there was a "pie in the sky, by and by" approach to preaching. The feeling was that things would get better—maybe not until we went to heaven—but someday they would improve. That underlying tone in preaching was: have hope because there is another life. Have hope because you won't always be in this life, and death will come as a friend to take you out of this impossible situation. That was the underlying theme. It was the scarlet thread that ran through African-American preaching prior to the civil rights movement. The civil rights movement caused African-Americans to focus on the fact that we had legitimate reasons to hope for a better life here and now. We expanded the old song that says "give me Jesus" to "give me Jesus along with some of the American dream." So African-American preaching began to help our people to refocus, not away from heaven, but toward experiencing racial and economic equality while living on earth prior to getting to heaven. Many times the pain of the struggle led to an overemphasis on the present experience of material gain. Theological extremism is the brainchild of heresy, and so I encourage and practice homiletical caution and integrity when preaching about prosperity and stewardship. I think that is the most significant paradigm shift that took place when we left slavery and Jim Crowism, entering into this modern era.

The Influence of Martin Luther King Jr.

Wiersbe: Did you see any difference between Martin Luther King Jr.'s preaching in a church setting and the addresses he gave as a civil rights leader?

Bailey: From what I've read about him, Martin Luther King Jr. had a real passion to preach.

Wiersbe: He considered himself first of all a preacher?

Bailey: Yes, he did; but so often this whole civil rights issue was so demanding upon him that even in his preaching he would gravitate toward the civil rights issues. From time to time that took him away from his original passion. Through reading his civil rights messages along with his preaching, I have not noticed much of what we today would call an evangelical emphasis. Most of his preaching characterized the social perspective of the gospel. I do think, however, that a strong gospel emphasis is there, because if the vertical Godward emphasis is right, the horizontal emphasis will also be right. Typically, I consider his bent was more toward the social aspects of the gospel than the evangelical.

Wiersbe: Was he imitated? Did the younger preachers follow his example, so that a whole generation was preaching that way?

Bailey: I think Dr. King impacted a whole generation by his preaching. How much deliberate imitation there was, only the Lord knows. Sometimes we unconsciously imitate the people we admire the most. There were many who imitated King's rhetorical style, but that's not the aspect I'm referring to. I understand the rhythmic hum in his homiletics, but more than that, they imitated his approach by addressing larger society and confronting it with the concepts of liberation from Scripture. African-American preachers support that emphasis. But more importantly and historically, the African-American preacher has always been a biblical preacher. Dr. King influenced them to include the social as well as the evangelical, but never to the extent that many people think today. If the truth were told, when Dr. King was alive he was not appreciated as much in African-American culture as he is today. Even some African-American leaders viewed him as a radical. Perhaps it was for fear of the position he took as well as for fear of unknown reprisals the opposing dominant community might inflict on our black community. Perhaps it was the inability to see the reality of the freedoms we currently enjoy today.

Wiersbe: Like Moses and Pharaoh?

Bailey: Absolutely. King was feared. Even in the city of Dallas, the black preachers organized to keep Dr. King from coming in the sixties. The black preachers were fearful because they had established certain relationships with the powers that be, and they did not want Dr. King's message of liberation to jeopardize or threaten those relationships.

Wiersbe: Does that situation still exist today?

Bailey: To some extent, those relationships today would be considered as politically correct.

Wiersbe: Uncle Tomism?

Bailey: Absolutely. Perhaps it was good for the leader but not so good for the cause.

Wiersbe: What were the black pastors preaching prior to the leadership of Dr. King?

Bailey: The dominant theme was a message of comfort. Once again, for sustainers, the message was hold on. But reformers were challenging the status quo of racial inferiority. For example, Bishop Henry McNeal Turner of the A.M.E. Church in 1898 was preaching the importance of black people's ability to see God and Jesus in their own image, as opposed to seeing God as a fine-looking, symmetrical, and ornamented white man. Many others such as Richard Allen, Henry Highland Garnett, and Alexander Crummell, to name a few, preached head-on against white supremacy. They, along with other reformers, paved the way for Dr. King's message. Manning Marable was correct when he suggested that the greatness of the African-American church comes from linking the spiritual strivings of the masses with a social commitment to challenge Jim-Crow laws, political disenfranchisement, and all forms of economic deprivation.

One-Sided Christianity

Bailey: We need to make some kind of case for *One-Sided Christianity*. Ron Sider is the author of that book. He has probably done one of the best jobs of showing that preaching the gospel involves more than just the salvation of the individual sinner.

John Stott, in his book *Involvement,* has really challenged the church, because he lays out—even for the evangelicals—this whole idea of a personal relationship with God and that the social appeal is the right biblical holistic approach. It has always been historical. Then he recalls the names of Finney, Whitefield, Hodge, Spurgeon, Wesley, and Edwards, who were heroes of the conservative movement of the eighteenth century, particularly in New England, and who all adopted a holistic approach in their ministries.

Wiersbe: Wilberforce and others had a holistic view of the church's ministry, but around 1900 the two aspects of the one message somehow separated. I think we have to help white preachers understand that what black preachers are doing is not inconsistent with white evangelical history. If anything, it's the black preacher who was consistent.

Impacting the White Pulpit

Wiersbe: I was pastoring in Kentucky during the sixties, and most of what I saw could be called retrenchment. The church I was pastoring was not officially integrated. People from other races attended, but integration was not a big thing on our agenda. Unfortunately, there were a few people in the community who were still fighting the Civil War. So we didn't see much social change. Ministers just kept on preaching their sermons and not making much of a social application. I probably should go to the altar and confess this sin myself, because I hardly acknowledged what was going on all around us.

But is there such a thing as "typical" white American preaching? Even today, one of the great influences on the American pulpit is the British pulpit. I wonder who in American preaching history was really the first American preacher who preached like an American? In the early years of our colonies, the ministers did traditional Puritan preaching, just as they had done in Britain. Perhaps our first truly American preacher was Henry Ward Beecher, and he had quite a social emphasis in his preaching. The Puritans were going to build the city on the hill and fulfill the great American dream, whatever that is. When our white congregations come together, I think that's the image that binds them together—the great American dream. Whereas in the black churches the overriding image may be deliverance from bondage, in the white churches the emphasis is on success and materialism, the great American dream.

Would Harry Emerson Fosdick's preaching be considered typical white American preaching?

Wiersbe: I doubt it. First of all, he was doing counseling on a group scale. He was a remarkable preacher who talked to the individual in the congregation, not to a congregation. He had a genius for anticipating objections and answering your arguments before you voiced them. But Fosdick didn't talk a great deal about race as such. He talked about unity and equality. He preached about America learning to be one people, but I don't know that he talked a great deal about race.

Bailey: No, he didn't, at least from what I have read, and I think I have all his books in my library.

Wiersbe: When Billy Graham insisted on integrated meetings, he upset many traditional evangelical people. Some of us remember when Billy Graham started with Youth for Christ in 1945, and of course, the historic Los Angeles crusade catapulted him into national prominence. He always insisted on integrated meetings, and he had men on his staff who were of different races. At least two of his associate evangelists were black.

What do you mean by "the first truly American preacher?"

Wiersbe: Well, I mean the preacher who dared to cut the British roots, not theologically but homiletically. I think Beecher may have been that man. He was a great man of imagination, and he didn't try to sound like Spurgeon or John Owen. I think money, comfort, protection, the great American dream—"Don't bother us, we're busy succeeding"—has been the emphasis in too many white congregations. In the past, the mainline congregations were criticized for not preaching the gospel but getting involved in social action instead, as if social action is contrary to the gospel.

Where Were the White Churches?

Bailey: That's one of the criticisms African-American preachers and churches have leveled, and continue to level, toward their brothers and sisters in the white churches. We do know from history that in the northern colonies, the Quakers attempted to evangelize slaves and end slavery largely through the work of John Woolman and Benjamin Lay. In contrast, the Puritans argued to evangelize the slaves but keep them enslaved. John Elliot and Cotton Mather sought to accomplish this by providing religious instruction for slaves. Moreover, the white churches in general, with few exceptions, did not come to assist the African-Americans in their struggle, particularly during the civil rights movement. Even now, white churches will call African-American churches to join them in their protests against abortion, and generally the answer they get is, "You didn't come to help us when we blacks were being 'aborted' by the system. Why should we come to help you when you ignored us?" The interesting thing is that African-Americans believe in the right to life as much as any white evangelical. But their unfortunate social experience causes them to refuse to be aligned even with churches of the same theological position as theirs that wouldn't stand with them in their hour of need. This decision has created misconceptions in the white community about the African-American church. "Why won't you join with us in our battles?" the white churches ask us. Then the white churches falsely conclude that apparently blacks are not being biblical or spiritual. Many white Christians don't understand that the social problems that resulted from slavery so injured African-Americans that they don't want to be yoked with people who refused to stand for equity, parity, and social justice. The question that my people ask the white churches is, "You're concerned about aborting people who haven't yet been born, but why aren't you concerned about people like us who are being 'aborted' economically, emotionally, psychologically, and socially after birth?"

People Who Shaped History

Often the story of our background centers on significant people who had a lasting impact. Who are some of the most important individuals or groups who shaped the history of the black church and its preaching?

Bailey: I don't know if some of the readers are going to like my answer. Marcus Garvey had a profound impact on my people. He founded UNIA (Universal Negro Improvement Association) in 1916. He was a nationalist and wanted to take them away from America and back to Africa. But he had a tremendous impact on both the theology and the sociology of black Americans.

What was his theology that encouraged him to promote this exodus?

Bailey: It wasn't necessarily his theology. Garvey believed that black people would never be respected until they had their own independent nation in Africa. It was his pragmatic and nationalistic thinking that impacted the theology of others. This included Frederick Douglass, who himself was a preacher and had a tremendous impact upon African-American preachers. Sojourner Truth impacted the northeastern revival movement along with women's rights by disarming challengers with wit and folk wisdom. Harriet Tubman was called the black Moses of our history because she led the Underground Railroad movement, which took African-Americans from the South to the North. She is given credit for leading three hundred to five hundred people out of slavery into freedom in Canada. She was revered and very beloved. From there, the late nineteenth and early twentieth centuries provide us with a roll call of excellence. We must not overlook the emergence of the "Black Social Gospelers," from Reverdy Ranson to Adam Clayton Powell Jr. You will find that Ralph Luker provides an excellent study entitled *The Social Gospel in Black and White.*

Wiersbe: There's a big time gap, isn't there?

Bailey: Yes, but in those days, people didn't really get a chance to live too long. If you recall, most of the men involved in seeking freedom for the slaves were killed. Once the leaders were identified as "rebels," they were removed. That was one way of discouraging anybody else from following his or her line of thinking or of acting. Three of the most renowned leaders of slave revolts, namely Gabriel Prosser, Denmark Vesay, and Nat Turner, were all hanged following their trials.

Training for Black Preachers

Wiersbe: What about schools? Most black preachers during the slavery era were called to ministry but not trained for ministry. At what point did schools emerge for the black preacher? Or did he just simply go to the white school? And if so, what kind of teaching did he get?

Bailey: We didn't go to the white schools. But the abolitionists did establish schools for blacks. That started happening during the post-Reconstruction era. Most of the schools that really made an impact were started sometime between 1850 and 1860. The school where I completed my undergraduate studies, Bishop College, is no longer in existence, but it started around 1880. You also have schools like Morehouse that go back to the mid–1800s. Schools were started primarily for religious purposes. Baptists in the North would establish schools in the South for black preachers. Then these schools began to move into teaching liberal arts as well. But that's the time frame for most of our schools. Most of our schools started in churches. So black education was really an outgrowth of the desire to train the black preachers and help them give the kind of indigenous leadership that was needed at that time.

Wiersbe: How did the black pastors and churches relate to the white congregations?

Bailey: Blacks had been attending the white churches, but Richard Allen led a movement out of those churches and founded the African Methodist Episcopal Church, which continues to thrive to this day.

Wiersbe: I spent five years at a seminary and never once was taught how to relate to the black churches and pastors in my community. Fortunately, I grew up in an integrated community. In high school, my locker partners were often African-Americans, and we got along fine.

Bailey: Black preachers were trained by our schools and experience to conceptualize the gospel. Even though he wasn't a preacher, William Edward DuBois was another person who had great influence in the African-American community. He was respected as a powerful thinker, and he often talked about the "two-ness" of people in America. I guess it's a concept that every race has to face, but it's particularly present with African-Americans.

Here's his idea: I'm an African and I'm an American, and I am constrained to live that out every day of my life. I have to recognize what this "two-ness" means in America. It's important for me to understand how to live in two worlds simultaneously. I must live in the micro black world, and I also must live in the macro white world. Well, that idea rolled over into our education and into our training. It also influenced our churches and the way blacks communicate. Even now, when I talk to the young preachers at our church, I tell them that they need to make certain adjustments if they're going to preach to a white congregation. Paul says it best by saying, "I become all things to all men so that I might win some."

Wiersbe: That's true of the whites as well.

Bailey: Sure it is, but we had to do that because our survival depended upon it. Your survival did not. You could ignore us and have a good life. If I ignored you, it might cost me my life. So, knowing this and looking up from the bottom, I had a much better understanding of how to deal with the people at the top than the people at the top had an understanding of how to deal with all of us at the bottom, because with them it wasn't a great necessity.

Immigrant Churches

Wiersbe: All of us came from immigrant ancestors. My mother's family emigrated from Scandinavia. My father's family came from Germany. Was there ever a time in the white church when immigrants came and found themselves in the same situation as you've just described? I'm referring to the problems like survival, communications, a different mind-set.

Bailey: Yes and no. Your ancestors were here because they took the initiative. My ancestors were brought here against their will. That's the difference. They didn't have a choice.

Wiersbe: Immigrant churches went on until pre–World War II. Swedish congregations sang in Swedish, thought in Swedish, while Dutch congregations did so in Dutch. Then as the older generation died off, the younger generation said, "We're not Dutch, we're not Swedish— we're Americans!"

Bailey: White people can blend in because the skin color is fundamentally the same. With my people the big difference was color, and because it could not be camouflaged, it was the source of our pain. It wasn't necessarily because we were from Africa, because white Africans could come to America and be accepted. Therein lies the difference. It was the color that created the problem.

Blacks Impact White Preaching

We've mentioned some of the individuals who have had a shaping influence on the black church and on black preaching. Have any of these individuals had an impact on the white church and its preaching?

Wiersbe: I think Martin Luther King Jr. may have been the first one. From what I've read, it seems there was "fraternal genuflection" every once in a while at special public occasions. The black preacher and the white preacher would participate in the meeting, like at the presidential inauguration, our great civil religious service held every four years. I started pastoring in 1950, so I've been an ordained minister over fifty years now. We white preachers knew the black ministers in town, we said hello to each other, but we didn't do ministry things together.

Bailey: Even before Reconstruction, during slavery, there were innumerable instances when the master would allow the black preacher on the plantation to preach not only to the blacks but also to the whites. In Methodist history, Harry Hosier (known as Black Harry), the assistant to Bishop Asbury, drew large crowds of white people during the first Great Awakening. John Jasper, who pastored the Sixth Mount Zion Baptist Church in Richmond, Virginia, saved special seats for "whites only." Even during Reconstruction, there were a number of times when blacks pastored churches where many whites also attended. In fact, as early as 1785 Lemuel Hayes became the first black pastor of a white church, in Torrington, Connecticut. Hayes was licensed in the Congregational Church in 1780. But the difference is that white America never allowed black preachers to affect their theology or their sociology.

Wiersbe: Perhaps this is true today. Back during the days of the civil rights movement, I was pastoring a Baptist church in the South. If I had preached a message dealing specifically with racial issues, some of the saints would have waited on me after the service to suggest that I not rock the boat. At that time some black leaders were visiting white churches and asking for "reparation money." The deacons and I discussed what we'd do if one of them showed up at a service. We decided that as long as the doors were open to everybody, we couldn't keep them out. If they had something to say from the Lord, we'd listen and consider it. I wasn't equipped to deal with those issues, neither in my training nor in my experience. I don't think I read a sermon by a black preacher until I was at Moody Church in Chicago. In our seminary classrooms we weren't introduced to black preaching.

Bailey: Gardner Taylor was known and appreciated for his great preaching by both blacks and whites. He is a bridge builder.

Wiersbe: He preached over the *National Vespers* radio program, made famous by Harry Emerson Fosdick. His messages were greatly appreciated by the listeners, regardless of race. Do you think Dr. Taylor's preaching is typical black preaching?

Bailey: It's not typical, because Gardner Taylor is not typical. He's unique. Fosdick's preaching wasn't typical white preaching either! Gardner Taylor came from Louisiana and lived through some very difficult experiences. He can tell you about his own struggles with racism and related problems. But he also has a real powerful testimony about how a white man delivered him from some Ku Klux Klansmen who were about to kill him. Of course, that affected his perspective that everybody is not like the Klan type. I've heard him preach when the message was very typically black, but his gifting is so unique that *typical* isn't a good word to use for his preaching.

The Importance of Understanding Background

Why is it important for preachers to understand their heritage? What difference does it make whether we know our history and background?

Wiersbe: Well, for one thing, you've got to know the mind-set of the people you're preaching to. If you don't how they think, how can you get God's truth into their minds? How do you get past all the fuzziness and even craziness that's controlling people's thinking? Plus, we never preach alone; we're part of a preaching history or heritage, a "great conversation" as it were. In the pulpit I may be a solitary person standing there, but I'm not alone. Every preacher is part of a preaching tradition that goes back for centuries. I'm glad that I'm learning to appreciate the black tradition in preaching because it's enriched my own ministry.

Bailey: When you look at the mega trends in America, you realize that by 2020 there will be a "browning" of America, so that preachers will have to learn how to preach cross-culturally, because America is changing. One of the places that we have to start is by learning what the genius of a people is— and this is particularly true for whites, because blacks have had to do it all along to survive. We need to know not only the history of the people, the core values of the community, liberation, and black history, but also what they bring to the table. What is the distinct contribution? We also need to know what mistakes we've made in trying to communicate with them.

For instance, there is a popular mistake that I frequently hear some white preachers make, when they say that black is the color of sin. Nowhere does the Bible say sin is black. If I as a black man hear that comparison, it impacts me negatively and might very well keep me from receiving the rest of the message. This error must be called to the preacher's attention. You have alienated me when you equated sin and blackness. I know that this is a cultural thing and not a biblical thing, but we still need to be made aware of things like that, so that communication doesn't turn into division.

We were taught in school to know the congregation and to study as much as possible the audience that you're going to speak to. So if you're going to preach and you have black people or members in your congregation, then there needs to be something positive said periodically from black history and culture so that we don't give the false impression that everything positive comes from Euro-America.

Getting to know the groups you are preaching to is so incredibly important. If you intend to preach to an integrated congregation, you have to learn something about African-American history and what contributions we have made. We have tremendous, gifted, and knowledgeable people that have affected events in our history, as well as today, and that previously and currently impact life for all Americans, black and white. It is imperative to learn that kind of thing. Use some positive illustrations from different cultures. You can't use them if you aren't aware of them. This isn't as much a problem for blacks, as a minority group, because we've attended majority schools. So we know your history, and we preach it with understanding, and we blend it in with our history as we preach. That needs to be realized in the white pulpit. White preachers should learn the value of what our people bring to the table and begin to do the same kind of thing that African-American preachers have done.

Wiersbe: When this "browning" takes place, will this be a new person? Will there no longer then be the two viewpoints, two cultures? Or will people select and maintain one or the other?

Bailey: From where I sit right now, I see a significant change taking place. I think the "browning" is symbolic of a social transformation. For instance, I'm a senior pastor with a number of people on my staff that are of other races. The secretary here is Hispanic, and I have two young white brothers on my staff. Ten, fifteen, twenty years ago that would have never happened. Not only because society would not have allowed it, but also because there has been an innate sense of superiority in whites that would not allow a white to work for a black man. I don't see that mind-set remotely present in these young white brothers at all. They actually think I've got something to offer them in their ministerial development. They believe they can learn something from me. They actually believe that. For someone who came up at the end of the Jim Crow movement, that blows my mind! I was never taught that someday I would be in this position and lead whites, Hispanics, and others.

When whites first started coming to our church, and ultimately when whites came on staff, people close to me asked, "How does a black man pastor whites? How do you supervise white staff people?" I replied, "Like I do anybody else." When I hired the first white staff member, a church officer complained because a black church was going to give a job to a white man. This is the mentality that we're dealing with.

With this new generation, something different is happening; our white brothers and sisters realize that there are African-Americans, like their white counterparts, who can spread an umbrella of leadership over them, and they can come beneath that umbrella and be a part of what's happening. That says to me that we've always had members of predominantly black churches joining white churches, but very, very few whites would join black churches. That's beginning to change. We even have Hispanics in the fellowship, and that represents another entirely different cultural perspective. They initially kept to themselves, but praise God, they are breaking out of that attitude.

Reverse Racism

Bailey: African-Americans sporadically have had problems with reverse prejudice and reverse racism. Now, in a church if I say something that's culturally negative about whites, I'll hear from them. For instance, I used to have a habit of saying "the other culture" and just left it. I didn't say white, just "the other culture." But it was clear to them what I meant, and they took offense to it. And they began to talk to me about that. "Pastor, what is this about?" They were very respectful, but they were letting me know they weren't into that kind of talk, and I changed. I haven't used "the other culture" in years.

Wiersbe: What do you say now?

Bailey: I try not to make any off-the-cuff comments that are negative. If there is an issue that I think whites need to take responsibility for, I just say it up front, but it's not like a backhand slap. That's what "the other culture" was, a backhand slap rather than facing the issue openly and lovingly. But now I'm preaching that God wants us to help develop a spiritual body that is cosmopolitan not only in its composition but also in its attitude. But there will always be some challenges as we do it, so why not face them head-on as Christians and see if we can work our way through it together?

Wiersbe: In other words, in the local church we don't set aside either black or white culture, nor do we necessarily blend both cultures. When I go to church, I'm not supposed to pretend that I'm not white and become something neutral, but rather I'm to see all people as Jesus sees them. When a black joins a white church, he doesn't forget he's black, nor is he given special treatment because he is black. The people of each culture must maintain their integrity and make their contribution to the ministry out of the richness of that culture. Am I right?

Bailey: You have to understand that in the black community there have always been people who didn't want to be black. During slavery there were two kinds of slaves: the "field Negro" and the "house Negro." That distinction was based on the texture and color of skin, and it created a conflict between the two groups in the African-American culture. They went to church according to their color, they lived and worked according to their color, and it has always been a divisive issue based solely on color.

I know a church that has the nickname "the blue-vein church." It's an African-American church, but you can't join it unless the color of your veins are literally visible. So the darker-skinned blacks call it "the blue-vein church." This means you must have a certain color to be accepted. They marry according to color, they get jobs according to color, and they associate according to color.

When the sixties came along with "black is beautiful," many black people changed their thinking about this idea of "classification by color," and it began to decline significantly. The concept still lingers with certain people, but it's nothing like what it was in the sixties, when that mind-set absolutely dominated the way people thought. Back then if you had blacks who didn't want to be black, they'd do almost anything to deny their heritage. There were blacks who wouldn't eat watermelon because of its so-called ethnic associations, and others said they detested chitterlings. These people would do nothing that carried any kind of ethnic overtones, because "white meant right." The white man's ice was colder, the white man's food was better, and if you wanted to succeed in life, you imitated the white man. Even in their preaching, they imitated the whites.

That concept moved into the church. A black man in a white church was really trying not to be black, so he made no black contribution other than the presence of his color in the congregation. In his thinking, his sociology, and his economics, he had already embraced the white world and abandoned his own world. Today we're seeing a resurgence and a rediscovery of the black heritage that once was abandoned. And blacks are learning to appreciate their own culture and contribution to the larger society. We still have churches that follow that pattern to some degree, but by and large it's changing. Because of the religious media, some blacks have been exposed to white preachers who expound the Bible. Once they get hooked on that approach to the Word, they gravitate toward white churches because that's where you can hear that kind of preaching. Perhaps they respond to the Word and are saved, but they stay in the white church. They stereotype their own people when they say you can't find expository preaching in the black church. They take for granted that all we have in the black community are preachers who are whoopin' and hollerin' and sweatin' and spittin', and they don't want that. But now that has changed to the point where whites are coming into predominantly black churches and feeling comfortable. The charismatic movement has had something to do with this change, because the expression of emotion in worship and in preaching has been generally accepted.

Wiersbe: You're right about that stereotype problem, because we have it in the white churches. The saying in seminary was that the black preachers had more heat than light, while the white preachers had light but no heat. The white congregations were "God's frozen people."

Bailey: There was a sort of anti-intellectual movement going on, but also a move toward bringing balance to black preaching. People are both cognitive and emotive, so let's pull this thing together and unite mind and heart. The black preachers were enabled educationally to minister to all people cognitively. These preachers were also maintaining the emotional side of their preaching and worship. Today it's coming together, and white churches are moving more toward expressing emotion more, while black churches are expecting some solid biblical content. We're seeing a balance between what you call heat and light, or scholarship and fire. Dr. James Earl Massey, who is dean emeritus of Anderson University School of Theology, says that churchgoers are more satisfied because the quality of preaching has improved and the tide is rising. Where we once had a generation marked by just a few pulpit giants, today a larger percentage of our ministers are being educated better, have greater resources, and are simply better preachers than ever before.

CHAPTER 2

ALIKE — EVEN IF WE ARE DIFFERENT

*A*s the conversation continues, we begin to explore what each community can learn from the other. Richard Allen Farmer has observed, "Rather than boasting that we are color blind, we will acknowledge the rainbow around us and learn from each hue. Rather than merely tolerating other cultures, which tends to be our posture, the future will cause us to celebrate diversity. . . . Our greatest peril may be our failure to appreciate the wondrous contributions of the people of color to the fabric of the universal body of Christ."[1] Yes, the church has diversity. But it also has similarities. What do black preaching and white preaching have in common?

Wiersbe: I want to start with a disclaimer. How much black preaching have we white preachers actually heard or even read? When you stop to think of homiletical history, it's difficult to say that this is a typical white approach or this is a typical black approach. There may be some major differences, but I have to be careful of accepting stereotypes.

Bailey: Well, it may be that the stereotypes were all you were exposed to.

Wiersbe: That's about the truth of it.

---

[1]Richard Allen Farmer, "African-American Worship," in *Experiencing God in Worship*, Michael D. Warden, ed. (Loveland, Colo.: Group, 2000), 129–30.

Stereotypes To Avoid

Bailey: I talked with my friend Dr. Stephen Olford about this matter of black stereotypes because he had a real concern about the emotionalism of black preachers. And he spoke about it in absolute terms. I said to him, "Your view just doesn't represent all African-American preaching." We must be careful about stereotypes, because the only exposure many whites have to black preaching is from what they hear on the radio and see on television. But the best black preaching may not be heard on the radio and seen on television. When I listen to some of these preachers on the radio, I wonder where in the world they came from.

I heard a black preacher on my car radio the other day, and I almost ran off the road. Sure, he was a black preacher, but his preaching wouldn't even be close to representative of the best of black preaching. This is true in many different cross-cultural and racial lines, black and white. We have to be careful what we mean by "black preaching" and "white preaching" and what is "the best" of either one. Fosdick said you don't judge music by rock and roll, but you have to consider Bach and Beethoven as well. You judge anything by what is the best.

Wiersbe: You always judge manufacturers by their best products, not their worst.

The Best of Both Traditions Are Biblical

Agreed. So looking at what we think is the best, what do black preaching and white preaching have in common?

Bailey: Well, I think it begins with the Bible. The best of both traditions are very biblical. The best of black preaching, and most of black preaching, has always been very biblical. The similarities today, I think, are focused on preaching for impact, results, and change, because that's what we are all attempting to do. We want to bring about changes in behavior and changes in the church and in society.

Wiersbe: But the black preaching community has constantly touched an area that the white preachers have avoided, namely, not only individual change but structural change. Very rarely would you find a white preacher applying the Word of God to the way city hall is working.

I had a long talk with a good friend of mine who pastored in a large city, and I kept bringing up the traditional white theology that says, "If you change the person, you will ultimately change the community." He disagreed with me. He said it wasn't enough just to change an individual here and there; we must also work to change structures in the cities. We have to change structures because the political and legal structures in these societies are built to keep down the poor man, the black man, and the disenfranchised. I asked, "How are you going to change these structures?" His reply was that we must change people's minds so we can change laws and build social and political structures that serve all the people equally. That means getting the right people in city offices and new ideas on the agenda.

Bailey: Some people vilify Reverend Jesse Jackson, but one of the issues he has addressed as a preacher and as a social critic is this whole area of structure. African-Americans by and large vote Democratic, because we believe in big government. Traditionally, most Republicans believe in small government. When you get past the theory and try to understand the practice, when you look at the human situation of African-Americans, you understand why we don't trust local government to change structures. Local government is more interested in perpetuating individualism and the status quo. It takes big government to do the job, because big government is more interested in helping the whole person in the whole of society. It sees groups as well as individuals. So in our black preaching and teaching, and in our values, we focus on whatever will help our people the most. This does not mean that African-Americans ignore moral and ethical issues; black preachers tend to speak out against all societal evils. We gravitate to a party that will address our local issue from the national perspective, to bring pressure on the locals to do what is right in bringing about equity and parity. The local political arena is not necessarily inclined to do these things unless something bigger influences them. Republicans believe differently, but Republicans aren't sitting where I sit. They don't need big government. It would be to their advantage, by and large, to have small government. But their philosophy serves a totally different purpose than what serves the people I serve as well as myself.

Wiersbe: Black preachers and white preachers start with the same inspired Word of God, but we don't look at that Word through the same eyes. Why?

Bailey: Because our historical and cultural experiences are so different.

Wiersbe: How do we change that?

Bailey: We cannot change our historical experience; however, we can work to change our cultural experience by seeing the value of cross-pollinating.

Preaching Personally and Socially

Wiersbe: It seems that the white preacher needs to be more sensitive to issues he may have tried to avoid. I've been preaching for over fifty years, and I look back and ask, "What have I been saying to people?" Well, I systematically taught the Bible, but I don't think I always applied that Bible to special areas of need in society.

Bailey: We need to have more conversations, seminars, and workshops designed by the driving forces that comprise and represent Christian leadership, theology, and preaching in our two worlds. We need to listen to each other and learn from each other.

Wiersbe: And maybe get pushed around a little and bruised in the battle. Too often the white preacher studies the Word of God and asks, "How can I comfort and encourage my people?" We hope to change people, but we don't want to stir up trouble. I once heard John Stott say, "Wherever Paul went there was a riot. Wherever I go, they serve tea."

Bailey: But effective preaching has to involve our personal experiences, and so the text must be studied from two different perspectives. The African-American basically comes
to the text from what I call the underside, while Euro-
Americans come to the text from the triumphal side of
the text, the topside. When I study the text, I look at it
not only from the viewpoint of my academic training and
reading—which has come primarily from the Euro-
American background—but also from the context of the
people I serve. I ask myself, "What does this text say to
these people who are the children and grandchildren of
slaves and who are still dealing with post-traumatic stress
disorders, injustice, institutional racism, and racial problems on a daily basis?" So I've got to deal with people's
spiritual, marital, social, economic, and psychological
problems, as preachers do everywhere, but more so as
the shepherd of people who are and have been disinherited and disenfranchised. Part of the reason for the
marital problems among blacks is that in corporate
America, the husband can't keep a job that pays a decent
wage. So my studies have to bleed over into their reality.
How can preaching help this person to confront and deal
with structures, systems, and people who either inten-
tionally or unintentionally participate in a system
designed to keep him down and restrict him? I must give
a word of Christian hope to help him and his family deal
with negative situations positively.

Wiersbe: But when a white preacher starts talking about changing
structure, and when God ceases to be a Republican or an
Independent, that preacher is in trouble.

Bailey: But God is changing a lot of them. I'm developing relationships with white pastors who are willing to take the
risk of getting put out of their churches for the sake of
truth, and I'm very encouraged, because I haven't seen
this before.

Wiersbe: In the white churches, congregations expect us to preach
personal principles, *personal* morality, and *personal* ethics,
but we must never apply these things to society and the
body politic. Keep everything individual! Now, I realize

that God uses individuals to get things done in this world, but didn't Jesus deal with some of the festering wounds of society when he was here on earth?

Some of the structures in Jesus' day were both political and religious. If he'd left those structures alone, he probably wouldn't have been attacked as he was.

We're warned not to preach politics. But Joseph Parker, in Victorian London, preached politics and even cursed the Kaiser right from the pulpit. Spurgeon was more involved in politics than people realize, and his convictions were liberal.

Bailey: Liberal and Conservative are helpful labels, but when you get right down to it, the main criteria is "speaking the truth in love" (Eph. 4:15). That love must be the voice of the voiceless, because there are those who don't always have the power to fight their own battles and get things done or move the hand of the majority.

Misleading Stereotypes on Content and Emotion

Wiersbe: One thing I've heard from some white preachers, even leading preachers, is that the black preacher is interesting to listen to, but he doesn't say anything. His sermon lacks content. The first time I heard E. K. preach, I said to myself, "This is a remarkable thing; this man is saying something solidly biblical, and yet he's doing it in an interesting way." He had excellent content, good exegesis, practical application, and a presentation that was interesting. After the meeting, I thanked him for preaching that way, and I may have shocked him. Now, why was I surprised that a black preacher actually preached from the Bible? Because I hadn't heard too many black preachers do that. I had this mistaken idea that all black preachers were interesting but didn't have much content. But let's confess that many white preachers have excellent content but are boring to listen to. Spurgeon said that many preachers are so dry that they would make good martyrs and would burn up quickly.

Bailey: The perception in black churches is that white preaching is unrelated, cognitive, and abstract. The white preacher lectures to the head but does not preach so that it moves the heart.

Wiersbe: The white preacher's approach is mostly cognitive, because we want to be good exegetes and "rightly divide the word of truth." But when the sermon is ended, nothing has happened. People go home with full notebooks and cold, empty hearts.

Bailey: Blacks expect the preaching to be a congregational experience. The perception in black churches is that you don't get that experience while listening to most white preachers in white churches. The white preacher's intent is to inform the head and not necessarily to move the heart and change the behavior. That's a general perception, I know, and I hope I'm not leaning on a stereotype. The white preacher seems to avoid the emotion that we believe is necessary if we're going to have the whole package. I admit that from time to time, honest emotion is different from shallow emotionalism, which is the manipulation of emotions. But emotion is a good thing. We have it in all parts of our lives.

Furthermore, white preaching is not political in the best sense, and therefore, it's irrelevant to the black community. Preaching has to be holistic for it to be relevant to us. If you're not addressing things that have to do with where I live, where I sleep, what I eat, what I'm dressed up in, and how I can get a job, then it's an irrelevant sermon. This includes matters related to race and racism. Historically speaking, the pulpit in the white church has been either in the forefront of racism or the defender and preserver of the status quo. Even worse, white preachers have totally ignored our problems, and blacks have taken an affront to that.

When People Talk Back

Wiersbe: One of the things that I like about the black church is the fact that the congregation is a part of the preaching. Now, worship in the white churches encourages participation and even enthusiastic participation, but when it comes to listening to the sermon, we close the books, open the Bible, and shift into a different mode.

Some folks at our church in Lincoln, Nebraska, have the video of the message that I gave on Hebrews at one of the expository preaching conferences sponsored by E. K. Bailey Ministries. One of the young men who had watched the video asked me, "What kind of a meeting was that?" I told him it was a great meeting and we had a blessed time in the Word. Then he asked, "Does it bother you when the people talk back to you like that?" I said, "Bother me? It's like pouring gasoline on a fire!" "Don't you lose your train of thought?" "No, not at all. I love it. The people encourage me to do better."

But when I preach in the average white church or conference, too often the people sit there with open Bibles and blank faces, and I wonder if they're really listening. Am I wrong in expecting a congregation to enter into the message and give some expression of what the Word is doing in their minds and hearts? When the black minister preaches and the congregation joins in with him, he's expressing for them ideas and feelings they may find difficult to express themselves. He speaks for God and also for the people. Am I on the right track?

Bailey: I think there's a combination of factors. The preacher is expressing what they find difficult to express themselves, but at the same time they are affirming the fact that the preacher and the people have entered into a sacred experience. It's a word of witness and a word of affirmation. The preacher is a voice for the voiceless in one sense, and they are rallying to their cheerleader. They're saying, "Yes, yes, yes! That's what we want to say, that's how we would say it. We just don't have the words to say it. So go ahead, preacher!" But at the same time they're saying, "Yes, I've experienced what you're talking about, and praise the Lord, you're right on!" The response can mean either "We agree" or "We've felt it"—one of those, but it is still a participatory moment.

Wiersbe: Over these years I've tried to be both a pastor and a preacher. I have friends who use the title "pastor-teacher," but there's no evidence they do any pastoral work. Theirs is a pure pulpit ministry. Do the black preachers, by and large, do pastoral work? I don't mean going from door to door looking for prospects, but mingling with the soldiers in the trenches.

Bailey: Yes, by and large, they do. But some of that is changing because of the influence of the multistaffed megachurches, where there are multiple ministries. Some churches today have grown too large for the pastor to effectively shepherd a congregation.

Chief of the Tribe

Wiersbe: But whether the church is large or small, pastors can still be with their people.

Bailey: Yes, but most of them don't. The reality is that most of them are not inclined that way. The whole megachurch concept is that you're no longer a shepherd, you're more of a CEO. Unfortunately, this removes from the people the shepherd image that they really need. In the black community, the chief of the tribe has always been the pastor. To a great extent, he's looked upon with that same tribal mentality. The chief was also the father of the community, the healer, and you brought all your problems to him. I believe we still have that approach, even with the size of our church. People share with me very minor, insignificant things as well as major things. That the preacher-pastor is the spiritual father and friend is still very much believed in our community.

Wiersbe: Would they accept somebody else after you left? I know a pastor who was very successful and stayed for many years in one church, but he was the chief. The members wouldn't buy a new car without consulting him. They wouldn't buy a house without consulting him. But as the church gets larger, what am I to be? A shepherd or a real estate agent? Do you have that happening?

Bailey: No. They wouldn't involve me in those kinds of decisions.

Wiersbe: They bring personal matters that affect their Christian life and their homes and so forth?

Bailey: Those things plus things in the community. There's always community involvement. If any of my people run into an issue out in the marketplace or workplace, they come to me and ask, "Pastor, what are the mechanisms in the community that can shed some light on this matter and help set it right?" All the time, our people are looking for somebody who is attached to Operation PUSH on a local level. I'm an officer in our local African-American Coalition, and stuff comes to us all the time and we have to address it.

Wiersbe: The average evangelical white preacher might be called liberal if he involved himself that way. I suppose he could get some of his concerned members involved. How do we get rid of this business of "passing by on the other side" and ignoring the needs? How does a preacher get involved in a Christian way in his community to help people—whites, blacks, or whatever?

Bailey: I'm reading a book on "core values" by Aubrey Malphurs of Dallas Theological Seminary, called *Values-Driven Leadership.* He talks about how a new pastor can come into a church and initiate the process of getting the church on the same page with his core values. Of course, that's a real challenge. The book talks about how to transition a church. One of the key essentials is the pastor's leadership ability and his ability to identify core values that include community and race. His task, through biblical leadership, is to find himself and the church on the same page of those core values.

Wiersbe: But social needs and problems are emphasized in the Bible. We read the Sermon on the Mount through "dispensational eyes" and explain away social responsibilities. We have ways of saying, "This doesn't apply to the church; it doesn't apply to our community; it doesn't involve me." African-Americans wouldn't do that.

Bailey: No. Not at all.

Community Involvement

Wiersbe: Why are white churches doing it? For protection? For comfort? For safety? How can a pastor change the situation?

Bailey: Well, a pastor should begin to talk with his church leaders in a nonthreatening way, just as we're doing now. That starts the process of eventually getting the leaders around a table for lunch and talking to us about these important issues. Changing the core values of a congregation is a process, and it takes patience. I would identify the movers and shakers in the church and, depending on what I was dealing with, meet with them every week, either one-on-one or in small groups. I would talk to them about changing the core values where the church is called to match what God says in the Scriptures, and after a few years there should be some kind of measurable impact. But before you can make some significant progress, God may have to take some of them to heaven.

Wiersbe: And while we're talking with the leaders, we're also talking to the Lord.

Bailey: Absolutely. I have never had to address the difficulty of white structure in a local church, so maybe I'm a little naive on what it takes to change things. I've seen white structures in a community, and I know how difficult they are to change. I can just imagine how difficult it would be to change structures and attitudes in a church. But at the same time, I think that you're not going to change anything unless you have the courage to confront it and the faith to believe that God's Word is not going to return to him void. We must be willing to pay whatever price is necessary to stand for our convictions.

Wiersbe: But the white preacher doesn't have the magisterial position that you have in your church.

Bailey: But a lot of them are "getting the guts." That's what I'm seeing. The younger ones are seeing that the pastor of a church needs to be more than a facilitator but also a leader.

Wiersbe: Well, they're going out and starting their own churches. I don't know what your students told you, but my students said to me, "I'm not going to go accept somebody else's problems. Let them fuss with their own problems. I'm going to go out and start my own church." And in that situation, of course, you are the leader.

A Good Preaching Experience

What is a "good preaching experience" in a black church?

Wiersbe: Number one, it's communal. It's not isolated. They don't sit and passively listen to an exposition. It's emotive and it's imaginative. The aim is to get to the goal, not to preach a great sermon. Coming from a white preacher, that's saying a lot!

Bailey: And you've done well, extremely well, considering you're not a black man.

Wiersbe: Well, I'm trying to learn. It's helped me tremendously to be broken out of the mold. I was trained to take a passage, exegete it, analyze it, find the key idea, and construct a sermon outline. But an outline isn't a message any more than a blueprint is a building.

Bailey: I think the African-American preacher, by tradition, has been taught to step into that text, internalize it so that the people who listen can experience it through you. You open your heart first and then you open your mind, then books, and then you open your mouth. To us, the preparation and the delivery are both incarnational.

Wiersbe: The "word becomes flesh" as the Spirit works in our lives.

Bailey: Historically, I consider this approach to be one of the long coats of black preaching.

Wiersbe: But where did the whites lose that?

Bailey: You'll have to tell me!

Wiersbe: Well, we must have had this approach at one time in our history.

Could you give us an example of taking a text, incarnating it, and becoming part of it?

Bailey: If I were planning to preach about John when he was on the isle of Patmos, I might take this approach. In my sanctified imagination, I would walk with John on the isle of Patmos and let him show me the ins and outs of that isle. Then I would begin to walk my people through various experiences and translate them into experiences they have in their own lives. Like John, we are isolated from the larger community, and in that isolation you face difficulties, but you also have times of peace. Further, you also experience many challenges. I would remind the congregation that I'm using my imagination and taking them to the scene with me. I want them to see the colors and hear the waves and see the sun rise over that island. Because I have "transported" myself there through the text, the people go there with me as I explain John's words. They see the text through me because I have stepped into that text and internalized it. I come to the pulpit and in an incarnational way open up my experience so that they are enveloped in the scene and identified with the message it brings. The reason for this is because they've already had a similar experience. So what I'm doing is using the Word to bring out the experiences they've had and to help them see the relevancy of the text to their life. It is the genius of exposition and application conveyed at times either by storytelling or direct exposition, and the utilization of imagination and creativity, that makes the text intimate and personal.

Is this approach something you were taught in school? Do you develop it intuitively by watching and listening? How did you come to this?

Bailey: Primarily by exposure to effective preaching. Yes, I've heard the great preachers do it. Sandy Ray, from New York City, used to say something like, "Always drive in the right-hand lane; you can get off easier." He told us to "preach in the right-hand lane because if you need to get off, you can always find an exit." This is using everyday realities to explain and understand spiritual truths.

Imagination versus Analysis

Wiersbe: Yours is a tradition of using imagination to package truth. The white tradition emphasizes analysis—taking things apart. I'm not sure we always put it back together again. There's an eastern proverb that says, "The great teacher is the one who turns your ears into eyes so you can see the truth."

Bailey: It is that kind of imaginative preaching that takes the everyday stuff of life and turns it into profound truth.

Wiersbe: But that's what Jesus did. We don't preach the way Jesus preached. If Jesus had gone to some seminaries—

Bailey: To say it facetiously, it would have messed him up!

Wiersbe: The Sermon on the Mount would begin with, "Now, as all of you know, there are five Hebrew words for worry." When I was teaching in seminary, I found that the biggest weakness in most of the sermon outlines I graded was information without imagination. They knew what the text said because they exegeted it. They knew what it meant because they knew their theology. But they didn't ask, "What does this text mean to me? What have I experienced that makes this passage alive to me?" Not only is the congregation left out of the text, but the preacher is left out as well. So then the sermon becomes informative and cognitive, but not interesting and compelling.

And the sermon is often emotionally sterile. It's for the head alone, and the heart has nothing to feel.

Bailey: Absolutely. That's one of the main problems with today's preaching.

Wiersbe: Have you ever been preparing a sermon and found yourself under such conviction you couldn't keep going, and you had to go straighten something out? I have.

Bailey: Very much so—especially with my wife! I've been preparing a sermon and have known I couldn't deliver the message because the conviction was so heavy, and even more, I didn't want to stand up, living a lie, while I'm trying to tell people the truth. I tell preachers that we can't fool our wives. They know. If you're out of sync at home, she may not say anything, but she's going to show it on her face. That look says, "How in the world can you stand up there and say that when you know what's going on at home?"

Wiersbe: If you read the average book on homiletics written for the white preacher, you won't find much said about weeping, crying out to God, cleaning up the act. I've written books on preaching and haven't said much about agonizing and internalizing. If a text grabs us, we need to let God break us and remake us through it. But we don't usually take that costly an approach to homiletics.

The Style of the Service

Wiersbe: Preaching is an act of worship, and the preacher whose attitude is "Let's get these preliminaries over with so they can hear me preach" doesn't understand this. I remember a well-known radio preacher, a friend of mine, who came to preach at one of the churches I pastored. He sat on the platform fidgeting and sighing and saying with his body, "When is this going to get over with so I can get up and talk?" But a congregation at worship is not "preliminaries." They are the people of God expressing adoration to their Lord, and that's what preaching is. When we preach, God is our number-one listener, and he knows our hearts.

I think folks in the black church are miles ahead of us, because they participate in the preaching and there's no break in the continuity of the service. In the average white church, we give, we stand, we sit, we sing, but when the preacher starts to talk, we no longer participate. That's wrong, dead wrong. So you're way ahead of us there. I don't know how to change it.

Bailey: It can't be something artificial. It must come from the heart. You can't organize it or legislate it. Worship is an act of the heart. Ironically, we as preachers find it difficult to worship while we wait to preach.

Wiersbe: I remember hearing E. K. preach to a predominantly white congregation. There were probably six or eight black preachers there. And he was preaching up a storm, but the congregation sat there quiet and respectful. Well, he stopped preaching, leaned over the pulpit, and said, "Man, that was shouting material."

Bailey: Now, I would do that at home, but to feel self-confident enough in a white context to say that has taken years of time, that's for sure.

Wiersbe: I felt like we in the congregation were smothering him. The silence was saying not only, "This is not the way we act in church," but also, "What's going to happen next?"

Bailey: For the worship to have symmetry, like a sermon has symmetry, the things that go ahead of the preaching are kind of like the introduction of the sermon itself. Martyn Lloyd-Jones didn't particularly like introductions, but I do believe a sermon needs an introduction.

But in addition to that, the worship, if it's going to have that kind of symmetry and theme and drive it home, needs to be reinforced by powerful Scripture reading, prayer, music—all of this building toward the experience of listening to the man of God proclaim the preaching event and invitation.

So it's thematically coordinated? Or isn't that important?

Bailey: Sometimes I think it is. A lot of our churches have not done that, but I think the more we do it, the more we reinforce the message. One thing I've picked up from white homiletics is to plan my preaching texts and themes months in advance. This gives the musicians time to get ready, and that helps to build worship symmetry. When we brought in a new minister of music a year or so ago and he began to plan this way, the people noticed it and liked it. Everybody is buzzing around the church about the way the invitation song coordinated perfectly with the sermon. It's just a matter of planning.

Wiersbe: But it takes skill to put together balanced thematic worship services. Choosing ten songs about love isn't the same as selecting songs that blend together but don't duplicate each other.

Bailey: There's a touching on the theme from different directions, opening different facets.

Wiersbe: That's right. But some preachers don't realize the difference between touching on a theme and boring people with the theme. Just because I'm preaching about faith doesn't mean that every song has to be about faith. There may be somebody sitting there who needs help in some other area of life. A balanced selection of songs can give that help to him. And if you're preaching Christ, everything touches life. Everything. I think planning a worship service is the most difficult ministry of the church. The preaching is hard enough, but planning that worship service is even harder, if it's done right.

The Length of the Sermon

How long should you preach? Historically, white churches have looked at approximately an hour for the entire service, maybe an hour and fifteen minutes.

Bailey: An hour for the whole service! In black churches, the service traditionally lasted approximately two to two-and-a-half hours! The younger generation, however, because of being influenced by thirty-minute TV shows and videos, are moving much more to the white framework. They still want the predominantly African-American style, but they want it done in the new time frame. Now, that's what's happening in our own community.

Wiersbe: I preach in some churches where they hand me a time sheet with every element of the service pegged to the last second. They give me twenty-four minutes to preach, not a second more. But what happens to spontaneity and the surprises of the Spirit?

Bailey: It's abbreviated or eliminated.

Wiersbe: So you have controlled spontaneity. That's a whole new approach.

Bailey: I'm telling you what's going on, not what should be. Sometimes spontaneity works havoc on the preacher, because he comes on nearer to the end of the service. So if the spontaneity comes during the time of the music and they don't want to cut it off, there goes the sermon. Sure, they want you to give your whole message, but they still want to get out at the same time. That means that we have to be more flexible. The older generation wants me to take my time and preach. To them, hearing the message is the highlight of the day. That's the zenith. They don't care what went on before that, if it takes me one hour to preach that sermon, they say, "Pastor! Stay with it!" I say, "Well, I've got to cut this." "Don't cut it short, pastor, we want the whole load." They're actually talking to me like that.

Wiersbe: Well, they weren't raised on sound bytes. Many of today's younger people have the attention span of a two-year-old.

Bailey: It's true that there's a different mentality there, but the younger folks are more integrated into the larger community than a lot of their parents and grandparents.

Wiersbe: Plus they're sitting there at computers and they're in control. The first time I preached at the Brooklyn Tabernacle, I asked Pastor Jim Cymbala how long I was supposed to preach. He said, "As long as you want to. Nobody's going anyplace." Their services often last over two hours. Nobody moves. Now that's an integrated congregation, with blacks, whites, Latinos, and various blends.

Bailey: That's not a typical church, by any stretch of the imagination.

Wiersbe: Jim tells me that when he goes elsewhere to preach, he finds it hard to fit into a straitjacket. A denominational leader asked him to be one of three speakers at an evening meeting, and Jim told him no. What if the Lord wants to break in on the meeting and turn it into a prayer meeting? What would the other two speakers do? Don't you find it difficult to use the scissors when you're a guest speaker but then on Sundays you have plenty of time to deliver your soul?

Bailey: Yes.

Wiersbe: And how has this affected you personally?

Bailey: It's a real challenge.

Wiersbe: Sometimes when we're really into preaching the Word in the Spirit, we learn truths in the pulpit that we didn't learn in the study.

Bailey: And with the African-American pulpit, it's even more likely to happen because the response of the people stimulates creativity on the spot. The interaction adds to the sermon. And that's a real challenge for me at our second service, which targets the buster generation. Interaction is being curtailed. But if I want them to keep coming back, I must make some adjustments. I have even added a question-and-answer period to the service, so I've certainly had to make some adjustments. I'm making adjustments because what we're doing seems to be working, and I want to keep it working.

Wiersbe: Do you ever stop a message and pick it up again the next Sunday?

Bailey: It's happened the last three Sundays, and because I'm in a series, I can do that. Usually the next week I'll review the previous message at the beginning of the sermon or else weave it into the body of the message. People who come back on Wednesday night also hear some of the previous message if I'm in a series. The idea is to feed the people and not just fit into a schedule.

Formal Training and Black Congregations

Some people have said that when African-Americans receive formal seminary training, they lose their ability to preach to a black congregation. They may end up preaching in the "white way." Is this a real or imaginary danger?

Bailey: For a lot of reasons, an emphasis on formal training can pose some real dangers. So my answer is both yes and no. African-American preachers are still going to college in record-breaking numbers, so our entire community is being educated along with the preachers. There's not the educational chasm between preacher and people that once characterized the community. There is a place, a niche, for both trained and untrained preachers, and people will gravitate to the preacher who communicates with them. That includes the style, values, even the educational training, that they appreciate. But I do think that if we're not very, very careful, the black seminary student in predominantly white seminaries can be robbed of his uniqueness as a black preacher.

Let me say it like this. I've seen African-American preachers go to white seminaries and digest Eurocentric concepts and come back misfits instead of ministers to the people.

They were "whitewashed," because they swallowed hook, line, and sinker the idea that black preaching, black history, and the black approach to ministry were worthless. So they abandoned their heritage and adopted the Eurocentric approach to theology, worship, and preaching.

I've seen others who have gone to seminary and it took five to ten years to "de-seminary" them, to make them fit to be able to communicate with their own people. So there are risks in going to some seminaries, and I've found that any school you attend has its baggage. You have to make your decisions wisely and decide what you can deal with. You take a rake and a pitchfork with you to pull what you need and pitch what you don't need. But I've also found that if an African-American preacher will stay in an African-American church while going through seminary, it takes less time to get "de-seminaried," because he kept his feet in the trenches. But a lot of seminarians use their training time as a kind of observation period, and when they come back home, they're out of touch with their own people. Staying in touch means you will know what the needs and problems are. You can lose what I call a knowledge of urbanology that's necessary for pastoral success. It has to be laced throughout your theology so that it can be proclaimed from the pulpit. You need a sense of what the urban issues are. If you go to some theological island while you're being trained, then you're going to be out of touch when you come back.

Wiersbe: That's even true of white ministerial students. Many times I've heard pastors say, "It took me ten years to get over seminary." I think one reason for this "peripheral education" that misses the essentials is that too many seminary instructors are preparing them for a church that doesn't exist, or an ideal church that will never exist. Some of the teachers are out of touch themselves because they haven't been in the trenches for years.

Training on Location

Bailey: I would like to see more churches provide practical training for their preachers.

Wiersbe: That's what they did in the early church. And that's the way it used to be in the early days of our country. An experienced pastor would take a student into his own home, teach him, and give him the opportunity to learn on the job. Today we call it mentoring.

If you could have a group of young men in your church and train them to preach, what would you do? How would you help them learn how to preach in a way appropriate for the black community?

Wiersbe: Throw them in the water and tell them to swim. Pray for them and with them. Pour yourself into them.

Bailey: There's a need for good balance. They need some exposure to preaching mentors. Booker T. Washington said that there is no education a man can get from a book that can compare to the education a man can get from another man.

At our church, if we know that a noted African-American preacher is coming to town, we call our preachers together and go to the meeting. Henry Mitchell came to Dallas to address a seminar at Southern Methodist University, and we had twenty-five of our young preachers go to hear him speak. Emmanuel Scott, E. V. Hill, anytime they visit our city, I'll call them and invite them to speak to our young preachers about preaching and ministry. The wealth of material that our young preachers are exposed to is tremendous, and just to rub shoulders with these godly men has been an incredible influence. Of course, they need opportunities to preach, so they preach in the preachers' meetings, and sometimes we will have a month of preaching in church auxiliary meetings. Every auxiliary is asked to invite one of the preachers to come in to preach a fifteen to twenty minute sermon. They don't get much opportunity in the public services because I do most of the preaching, and I have a very strong preaching staff. But periodically on Sunday nights, the "preacher boys" will get exposure.

Wiersbe: Are there other black churches in the greater Dallas area that know about the availability of these young men?

Bailey: Yes. I've been in the city for over thirty-six years, and I'm not the godfather, but I'm moving in that direction. Churches are calling to ask me to recommend preachers. I have sixteen ministry sons in the Dallas–Fort Worth metroplex, all of whom started preaching in this church. Also, a church might ask me to lead them through the process of calling another preacher. Well, that means at least once a month one of my preachers goes over and preaches. So yes, the Lord does open doors. As other churches have seen the "success" of our church, then they call on me to ask for help.

Wiersbe: So you've become a bishop in the biblical sense.

Bailey: There are still a couple of preachers ahead of me—we call them godfathers. It's a secular term, you've got a biblical term—but they're well up in age. One of them is close to ninety, and at this time he's still pastoring and preaching. But some of the overseeing for the traditional Baptist churches in the city seems to have fallen in my direction.

What We've Learned from Each Other

If you had to single out two or three valuable insights you've learned from the other community, what would they be?

Wiersbe: Well, first of all, I'm learning that the whole person has to be in the pulpit. If your heart's broken, your heart's broken. If you're going to cry, you're going to cry. If you're going to shout, you're going to shout. The tradition I was raised in didn't take that approach. You were a persona in the pulpit, not a person. In other words, be yourself, be your best self, and have the whole person in the pulpit.

Second, the importance of the congregation in preaching, not just as listeners but even more so as participants. The main metaphor for most white preaching is that of a conduit or a conveyor belt. The preacher's in the pulpit, and the congregation is sitting out there before him. There's a conduit or a conveyor belt between his mouth and their ears, and he loads this conveyor belt with all kinds of stuff for their good. But preaching doesn't work that way. I've learned that the people must be a part of the preaching process, in the preparation, in my praying over the message, and in my delivery.

I think the main thing, though, is the need for a godly imagination. It was a complete liberation for me to discover that imagination is a gift of God and that people are using it all day long. Disney made a fortune out of using imagination, and the church ignores it. So I think those three contributions have been the most to me.

Bailey: Foremost has been the importance of scholarship. Because of the academic poverty imposed on our people, for years we were denied the education and training we've needed. It's necessary to do research and to strive to be accurate in your interpretation of Scripture. We need access to the resources that are available so we can study the great pulpiteers of history. All of this is very important to blacks in the development of their thinking and telling of the good news. That's the most important thing I think we've learned from white preachers.

Wiersbe: Something has been going through my mind, and it may just be a detour, but here goes. The black approach to preaching and to worship seems to emphasize the immanence of God. God is our friend. I am worshiping him and he's near me. In our traditional white churches, it's the transcendence of God that is emphasized. God is "up there" and worthy of our worship. That's probably an oversimplification, but doesn't each outlook affect our preaching and worship differently?

Bailey: Yes, we see it both in preaching and in our gospel music, because until recently, gospel has been very unique to the black church. What we had to watch out for was an overemphasis on *my* experience and not enough emphasis on the transcendence of God. That message was left to the anthems and the choir. Our experience is more compatible with immanence—God is with us—so we have to be careful about overdoing it, but that certainly has been a focal point of both the music and the preaching.

Wiersbe: But if our experience dictates our theology, it could be dangerous. Nothing should supersede the theology of Scripture. Bishop Hanley Moule said he'd rather tone down a fanatic than resurrect a corpse. But why should we have to choose between the two?

Bailey: Again, the key is balance.

As we have seen, this conversation reflects some of the differences that exist in the two communities. Dwight Perry says, "The preaching style in a black church may be very different from that in a white church. But each is valid and each makes an important contribution to the body as a whole." He concludes, "Paul wrote about this in 1 Corinthians 12, where he said that the parts of the body are different but each part is invaluable to the whole. The black style of worship is part of God's sovereign, diversity-packed plan for his church."[2] Yes, we can learn from each other.

---

[2]Dwight Perry, *Breaking Down Barriers: A Black Evangelical Explains the Black Church* (Grand Rapids: Baker, 1998), 101.

CHAPTER 3

THE PERSONAL PREPARATION OF THE PREACHER'S HEART

F rom the first he fed others by what he himself was feeding upon. His preaching was in a manner the development of his soul's experience. It was a giving out of the inward life."[3] So Andrew Bonar described his friend, the famous Scottish preacher Robert Murray M'Cheyne. Preaching involves far more than simply mastering exegesis, hermeneutics, and communication theory. It begins in the prepared heart of the preacher. So with fresh cups of coffee in hand, we continue our discussion by focusing on the character and the spiritual life of the preacher.

Bailey: The great temptation we face is to attempt to do spiritual ministry in the energy of the flesh. It's a sin that's hard to identify. Our people sometimes detect that something is not right, but they don't always know what's wrong. When the preacher ministers in the energy of the flesh, he is spiritually dry. Since the principle is that everything produces after its own kind, we end up reproducing what we are. If we're spiritually dry as dust, you can only communicate dry as dust to a congregation.

---

[3]Andrew A. Bonar, *Memoir and Remains of R. M. m Cheyne* (London: Banner of Truth Trust, 1996), 36.

Jerry Vines says that the Spirit of God is the needle that pierces the cloth of the heart that makes room for the gospel thread. So people are not changed by my eloquence. They're not even changed by my knowledge. They are impacted first and foremost by the power of the Spirit of God. If the Spirit does not penetrate the heart, then the knowledge, the information, the eloquence, accomplish nothing, and our preaching is in vain.

The anointing of the Spirit must be upon the preacher before it can penetrate the heart of the listener. It is the power of the Holy Spirit that brings about personal regeneration and transformation. Dr. James Forbes Sr., senior minister of the Riverside Church in New York City, says his understanding of the anointing is the experience of the presence of the Spirit. And if we prepare and preach out of that experience, we will have nurturing from and collaboration with the Spirit, so we can expect to receive the text and message that is sent by God.

Presently I'm preaching through the well-known "Prayer of Jabez" on Wednesday nights, and I'm at the point where it says, "Oh, that Thy hand will be with me." Jabez had been blessed. His borders had been enlarged. Now he was at a fork in the road. Would he travel the road of dependence, or would he travel the road of independence? That's a choice every preacher has to make, especially those who have seen God's blessing and have experienced the enlargement of territory.

Stuart Briscoe comments that high visibility is always accompanied by high vulnerability, and the preacher, like all others, is highly vulnerable to his own successes. The temptation of the flesh is to be proud of what God has accomplished through you. You must continually stay before the Lord in prayer, genuinely giving God credit for what he is doing in your life. In the Bible, the hand of the Lord is symbolic of the Spirit of God at work in someone's life.

Just as Jabez prayed that God's hand would remain on him, the preacher must also constantly pray for the Holy

Spirit of God to convict him of those debilitating sins of pride, self-centeredness, and arrogance, etc. How easily these sins come along to derail our spiritual progress! Prayer is vital so that we may remain humble enough and spiritual enough to effectively communicate the gospel of Christ to a spiritually hungry congregation. Prayer keeps us spiritual enough for the Holy Spirit to illuminate our minds and hearts so we can not only see the truth of Scripture but be able to effectively communicate that truth to the people as well.

In addition, we need to depend upon the Spirit to enable us to model Christ as servants of God. Our example teaches our people how to function either in the flesh or in the Spirit. One of the obvious signs of functioning in the flesh is that you don't really have a passion for an intimate relationship with God. At times we don't demonstrate to the people that it is his truth we're communicating, that our thoughts have been illuminated by the power of the Spirit of God and his truth is what we're communicating.

One of the greatest temptations that any seminary-trained preacher faces is depending on our training, our experiences, or our gifts and abilities instead of depending totally on the Lord to use these things for his glory. According to Galatians 5:17, we are a combination of spirit and flesh, and they constantly war against one another. There is an old adage that says we have two natures, and the nature you feed is the one that wins the battle.

Wiersbe: Years ago I heard A. W. Tozer say, "If God were to take the Holy Spirit out of this world, most of what the church is doing would go right on and nobody would know the difference." I agree with that wholeheartedly. I thank God for the four years I served in Youth for Christ with people like Bob Cook, Torrey Johnson, and Ted Engstrom. They kept reminding us that if we could explain what was going on, God didn't do it. Bob Cook would often end his prayers, "Oh, Lord, keep this ministry on a miracle basis." Now, that's not an easy way to live, but it was the way Jesus, the apostles, and the prophets lived, from one miracle of God's grace to another.

Few things are more dangerous to ministry than trying to impress people so we can enjoy hearing the compliments. The Spirit glorifies Jesus, not us. The Scottish professor James Denney said, "No man can bear witness to Christ and to himself at the same time. No man can give the impression that he himself is clever and that Christ is mighty to save." We end up being controlled by what people want and thus living at their low level. At the same time, we must not become spiritual snobs. The Lord has a way of disciplining us when we need it. You get to thinking you've arrived and then, zap, you wake up in the hospital. I'm glad the Lord has a loving way of working with his servants.

But the black pastor seems to have more authority, or at least higher stature or status, than the white pastor. Does this present a greater temptation? I go to a board meeting and when it's over, I might come out licking my wounds. The black pastor is revered as the leader, God's man in the church.

Temptations of Leadership

Bailey: Every leader, regardless of race, creed, or color, has his own set of temptations. Leadership is always under attack, whether it is in government, business, education, or the church. In African-American churches, the privilege of being the senior pastor, with the kind of influence that it brings, has its own set of temptations. The pastor who has the kind of influence that we have may be tempted to be an autocratic leader. Pride expresses itself in different ways. But in the end, the basis of the problem is the flesh. These temptations are manifestations of the sin nature, according to our own temperament and what struggles we have individually. So, to answer your question, the African-American pastor may face greater temptation in this area simply because he has greater freedom.

Wiersbe: Who is the pastor's pastor?

Bailey: Unfortunately in African-American churches, most of our pastors don't have a pastor. It's tragic, because it helps to breed problems like the lack of accountability in moral issues, in professional issues, in study, and in family life. It's an unfortunate situation, but it's true that many preachers in the buster generation don't have a desire for accountability.

Wiersbe: Because?

Bailey: Well, I suppose it's because they think they know all they need to know.

Wiersbe: Nothing really happened before 1980?

Bailey: Right. They were born with the gift of omniscience, so they don't really need a pastor. I teach a pastors' forum once a month, and I've invited some men in their late twenties or early thirties to join us. And they have rejected the invitations. Their attitude says "I know" and "I don't want to be obligated to anyone." They misunderstand my motives. Maybe they think I want to pastor their churches through them. I believe I'm called to minister to pastors. I know it's part of my calling, and so I reach out, but some of the young men aren't remotely interested in having a seasoned pastor help to develop them and hold them accountable.

Wiersbe: Of course, whatever they don't know, they can find by surfing the Internet.

Bailey: Well, most of the academic information they can find online, but not the practical things that come out of suffering and experience. Practical people skills aren't found online. And when they get into a difficult situation, they need a spiritually minded mentor who can skillfully walk them through it. They won't find that online either.

Are there any other temptations that preachers face?

Wiersbe: Well, there's always the temptation of preaching beyond our experience and sounding like we are a modern version of Peter or Paul. E. K. already mentioned the fact that you start believing what people say, and that's dangerous.

What about the temptation to recycle sermons rather than plow new ground?

Wiersbe: I see nothing wrong with recycling my sermons as long as I'm growing myself and not looking for excuses not to study. I went through one of my notebooks the other day and pulled out a half dozen messages that I've decided to work on and improve. I see nothing wrong with that. If a sermon is worth preaching once, it's worth preaching a hundred times, if you adapt it to each congregation.

Bailey: We'd better beware when we're not growing spiritually and plowing new ground, because then we're tempted simply to regurgitate what somebody else has said. Sometimes it's just the preacher's laziness, and sometimes they allow their schedules to get so full that they don't have the time to study. Remember the old motto: "Beware of the tyranny of the urgent." Well, the urgent becomes more significant than the important.

At our church, so much goes on that I have to get up very early to study. In the early days, I could start at eight o'clock and stay in my office at home until noon. I did that for maybe fifteen or twenty years, but things exploded when our church relocated. Because the mere size of the church doubled and even tripled, the demands were greater. Now I'm up before day to get the quiet time to meditate, pray, and study, to continue to plow new ground. What I'm saying is that some people don't make that kind of adjustment because they feel as though it's too costly and demanding.

The Right Priorities

Wiersbe: One of the key issues in any pastor's life, actually in any Christian's life, is maintaining the right priorities. Our first priority is our walk with God. The most important part of our lives is the part that only God sees. It is remarkable how many pastors get nervous when you start talking this way. Priority number two is the home, the family. Anybody can preach in my pulpit, but I'm the only person who can be the father and the husband in that home. The third priority is preaching. The mail can stack up as far as I'm concerned. I'm going to prepare a sermon.

Bailey: I agree wholeheartedly.

Wiersbe: When we were pastoring in Chicago, we were invited to be part of an evangelical fellowship of good people who got together on Saturday evenings. Well, Saturday is right before Sunday, and Sunday was a demanding day. My messages were completed by Friday noon, by the grace of God, but I used Saturday to prepare myself. I'd stay home and take time to prepare my own heart and mind for the Lord's Day.

Bailey: You have to give the Lord a rested body and a prepared mind as well as a prepared message.

Wiersbe: That's right. The average church has no idea the cost of preparing a message that is God's message. We're both at the point where we could take any passage and outline it. But an outline is not a message. That's the hard part. If all that was required in preaching was the outlining of a passage and the sharing of the outline, that would be easy. But that's not what real preaching is.

Bailey: One other temptation that you touched on just a little bit but I want to embellish. How shall I say it? When ministry becomes more important than your walk with the Lord. When you define who you are by your activity rather than your relationship with the Lord, there's trouble ahead. Warren's entire "Be" series of Bible studies puts the focus on *being* rather than *doing*. We live in a performance-oriented society. We worry about our image, what we have done, and not what we really are. In ministry there's a great temptation to *do* ministry without the underpinning of a solid relationship with God. This leads to that "sinkhole syndrome," when all of a sudden the ground caves in and everybody wonders what happened. But the decline has been in process all along because we didn't keep that strong walk with the Lord over a long period of time. Instead of a blowout, there was a slow leak.

Wiersbe: We remember that ominous statement about Samson: "He knew not that the Lord had departed from him."

Bailey: I just preached that text—Judges 16:20.

What kinds of things might preachers do during the week? What about Sunday? Is there preparation on Sunday itself? Is there anything to avoid?

Wiersbe: I think the most important thing we ever do is meet the Lord every day, that constant abiding in the Lord, reading the Word, praying. I think every once in a while we need to get away for a special retreat. Some churches give their pastor a study leave twice a year so he can get alone and study and think. There are many retreat centers available these days, and they aren't expensive.

Bailey: I agree that meeting the Lord every day is the primary way of preparing to preach and preparing the heart of the preacher. But after that, it comes down to a matter of discipline, setting sensible priorities, scheduling time wisely, and planning ahead—all of this is very, very important.

Wiersbe: Yet we should be willing, if necessary, to break into the plan if God moves us that way.

Bailey: But only if it's necessary. First you have to have a plan. However you come up with your preaching texts and themes, you need to develop a specific plan for turning ideas into messages. I have a file folder for each sermon idea. I develop a file on Scripture and subject, and I file my ideas away. Afterward I go back and develop the direction the sermons should take from the text, and then I begin developing outlines. I begin to do research on at least two months of that material and file that away. Every minister will have his own approach, but you must plan your work and work your plan.

Wiersbe: That's a lot of research!

Bailey: I have two research assistants on staff, and I tell them the direction that each sermon is taking. I give them the outlines—even down to the subpoints—and ask them to bring back to me what helpful material they find. I file all that away. It was early in December, and I was looking at the January calendar. Because I had a plan, I began to work on the first two or three sermons for January, and I finished them. So you must have a plan. Now, like you said, when something comes up that you have to interrupt that plan, it's not a problem. You just pick it up the next week and keep going.

Wiersbe: And the "interruption message" means more because it has a sense of urgency to it.

The Experiences of Life

Wiersbe: I can't speak for anybody else, but every experience of life helps me preach. You face emergencies of all kinds—personal, family, church—and they become opportunities for learning and growing. If we're walking with the Lord, even the family problems become something God uses to talk to us. Writing works the same way. Whatever happens to you can become a part of your growing and developing. When we get too busy and destroy the margins in our lives, our fires of creativity start to die down. We don't have to read the latest books or attend the latest seminars. The words of Nehemiah come to mind: "I am doing a great work, so that I cannot come down" (6:3).

What reading or music has helped nurture your own soul? What have you found most helpful to prepare your own hearts so you're ready to go into the pulpit?

Bailey: Well, I enjoy riding around, and because I am frequently in the car, I use that time to rehearse my daily devotions and offer praises to God as I am going from place to place. Also, because I travel so extensively, I have the opportunity to meet and interact with people and therefore increase my understanding of the prevailing trends and the culture in which I minister. I keep gospel music in the car, and it helps to keep my soul sane. It keeps me focused on God rather than on the stuff that comes over the radio, because we are inundated with billboards and other subliminal messages. I don't watch a lot of television. So I think that Christian music is very helpful in maintaining focus on God.

Wiersbe: I prefer to be alone with uninterrupted time to "digest" my message. I sit outside if I can. People think I'm loafing and staring into space, but my inner person is exercising.

How do you integrate into your own life what you preach, so that when you're in the pulpit, you're really ready?

Bailey: I think it's the reverse. You integrate it and then you share it.

Wiersbe: You'd better study and assimilate the truth before you walk out. I have a preacher friend, who is in heaven now, who used to preach himself under conviction and be the first one at the altar. After a few months of that kind of behavior, I would lose confidence in his ministry. I'll confess that I've prepared sermons I couldn't preach. They were just academic, good outlines, but it wasn't a message that had made a difference in my own life. It was just, you know, you have to say something. On the other hand, there are times when you are just so full of what God wants to say that the outline gets in your way.

Bailey: I haven't thought this through, but allow me to wonder out loud. I think preaching is more powerful when the preacher has experienced what he is preaching about. When I've attempted to preach something that I really have not experienced, I've seen God in that very week give me the experience that I needed.

I remember one of the first times I was going to preach on forgiveness, and I had announced it to the church two weeks in advance. That very week a dear friend betrayed me, and I cried all week long. If I had not announced the theme of my message to the church, I would not have preached it. I went to that pulpit teary-eyed—this was twenty years ago, and I can still feel the emotions now. God moved so powerfully through that sermon that people began to open up and start weeping and confessing their own need to forgive and be forgiven. This happened because God gave me the most painful experience of having to forgive a friend as I preached on forgiveness. I vowed I would never announce another sermon again.

I said I'd never preach on forgiveness again, but of course, I've preached on forgiveness several times since then.

Wiersbe: Consider the biblical examples. God told Jeremiah to preach messages about Israel's unfaithfulness to the covenant. Israel was God's wife, but she was a harlot. Then God told Jeremiah that he was not to get married. There's a price to pay to preach a sermon. Or take the prophet Hosea. One of my students handed in an outline on Hosea with the title, "You Married a What?" Hosea's wife became a harlot, and he had to publicly buy her out of the slave market! Think of what he had to go through to be able to preach forgiveness. Consider Ezekiel. God told him his wife would die and that he should preach a message based on that crisis. Talk about the price of a sermon! A person can teach algebra or repair automobiles and not have to suffer to do his job. But when it comes to ministry, the preacher is a part of the message, and sometimes he has to study his text in the furnace of affliction to find out what it means. Before I was married, I was an expert on building a home and raising children. But it was hollow. I didn't know what I was talking about.

Bailey: Preaching divorced from experience is just simply academic jargon. It's abstract, cognitive idealism with no power.

Wiersbe: I think the closest modern analogy to what Jesus meant by "disciple" is "apprentice." Not the Jewish idea of a disciple who sits and listens to a rabbi, but an apprentice who lives with the teacher, watches him, learns from him, obeys him, is encouraged to do well, and is corrected when he makes mistakes. That's what Jesus did with his disciples. They lived with him. They watched him. They went out and did what he commanded, came back, and told him how things went. A preacher is an apprentice, and if I'm not a part of the message, I'd better keep my mouth shut.

The Priority of Prayer

What is the role of prayer in preaching, both prayer by the preacher and prayer by those interceding for the preacher?

Bailey: Well, I think that prayer plays, obviously, a very significant role. But first and foremost, prayer is an act of worship.

Prayer is an act of dedication and rededication. Prayer is an act of communication with God. Prayer is an act of warfare. As you understand that you are involved in spiritual warfare and that our weapons are not carnal, you depend more and more on prayer. There are several weapons the Lord gives us to help us to be successful in the warfare, and heading that list is prayer. Immediately following that is the Word of God. A preacher by the name of Warren Wiersbe said that your spiritual life will never rise any higher than your prayer life. So prayer is our measuring rod for where we will allow God to take us in the work of building his kingdom.

Wiersbe: Do you ever silently pray while you're preaching?

Bailey: I have prayed while I'm preaching.

Wiersbe: There have been times when I have just cried out for help. I'm sure you've had the same experience, you just cry out saying, "Dear Lord, I'm not getting it across! It's just not coming through! Help me!"

Bailey: Well, I've asked the Lord to keep my mind on course. Preaching without notes demands concentration, and you run into situations when either your body isn't functioning normally, or your mind is not clicking, or you can feel the satanic opposition coming, so you talk to God and say, "Lord, hold my mind steady, relax me." Yes, your heart prays all the way through the message.

Wiersbe: The Scottish preacher Robert Murray M'Cheyne used to write prayers in the margin of his outline, things like, "Help, Lord!"

In the black church is there any custom of the church leaders meeting with the preacher to pray before the service? Are there any special ways by which you encourage your people to pray for you?

Bailey: Our prayer ministry at the church includes a number of things. We have thirty men whose responsibility it is to pray daily for the pastor. We have a group of men who pray together every Sunday morning prior to each service. We have a small group of men, four to five, who pray during the service, especially during the preaching. Then there are one or two men who will always come in, laypeople as well as leaders, who lead the preachers in prayer when we get ready to go out. Some of the laypeople will usually do that. So the prayer emphasis is real strong, and in most African-American churches they might not do it the same way we do, but there is a group assigned to pray prior to going out to minister.

I meet with this pastor's prayer team once a quarter for breakfast or for lunch, and I share with them my vision for the church, my personal needs as a man, as a father, as a husband, and as the pastor. They will take those needs and pray over them for the next quarter. They pray faithfully over them. I have walked them a little bit through Maxwell's book *Prayer Partners with the Pastor*, and of course, I'm constantly giving them information on what they can read about how to pray. We read through Dick Eastman's book *The Hour That Changed the World* and, of course, *Fresh Wind, Fresh Fire* by Jim Cymbala. As God would have it, I was in the middle of that book when the doctor told me I had cancer. Had I not been reading on prayer and practicing what I was reading, that news would have been the equivalent of Mike Tyson hitting me with a straight shot full-force on the chin. But because I was practicing what I was reading and enjoying it, when he told me I had cancer it didn't knock me out, and I was not completely devastated. The prayer focus provided supernatural strength to help me combat the life-threatening news.

Wiersbe: Jim Cymbala's books have also helped my prayer life. Two more of his titles are out—*Fresh Faith* and *Fresh Power*. I find it very helpful to do what Isaac did, redig the old wells. There are maybe a dozen classic books on prayer and the spiritual life in my library, and every once in a while I go back and read them again. *The Imitation of Christ* by Thomas á Kempis is a deep well of truth and blessing. So are the books by E. M. Bounds.

Bailey: Our prayer coordinator is a fan of E. M. Bounds.

Wiersbe: Rereading *The Pursuit of God, The Knowledge of the Holy,* and *The Divine Conquest,* all by A. W. Tozer, always does my heart good. I also like to read sermons, not to learn how to preach but to learn how to live for God. I turn to Charles Spurgeon, Campbell Morgan, George W. Morrison, and F. W. Robertson, among others. I find that when I get away and read these basic books, it gives me a new influx of joy and power. I have to confess I don't read the bestsellers, the books of the hour. I read the books of the ages.

Bailey: The great challenge for preachers is to do more than talk about prayer or even preach about prayer. We need to pray! Because we all can read books, but similar to many laypeople, we're guilty of talking about it when we seldom engage in the glorious practice.

Wiersbe: I learned something in Youth for Christ from Bob Cook, who was a great man of prayer. He taught us to pray when people least expect it but need it. A Christian brother comes to your house and fixes something, so before he goes, you pray with him. This is a great way to witness. Unconverted people start unloading their problems on you, so you ask if it's okay for you pray about it right then and there. The greatest thing about prayer is that you can do it anywhere, under any circumstances. I've prayed in an ambulance while I was near death. You can also praise God.

Bailey: You can pray on the treadmill.

Temptations

Suppose you had a chance to sit down with a young person who senses a call to a ministry of preaching. What kind of counsel would you give that person as far as guarding his heart?

Bailey: Solomon said it best: "Keep your heart with all diligence, for out of it flow the issues of life" (Prov. 4:23). Just as you give your whole heart to your wife and keep it that way, so we give all of our heart to the Lord. Your wife won't be impressed if you tell her that you are 90 percent faithful to her.

Wiersbe: I have a concern for my peers, those who were trained in the 1940s and '50s, as I was. Do you have contact with any of these pastors?

Bailey: Sure.

Wiersbe: What's their number-one problem? Has anything impacted you on that?

Bailey: Well, age is no preservative against sin, and there are temptations in maturity just as there are temptations in immaturity. Probably the number-one challenge that goes along with getting older is the inability to change your methods and approach while maintaining the message.

Wiersbe: That's exactly what I would say. As I minister from place to place, I run across my peers and find them bitter and angry and miserable because "it's not being done right anymore." One blessing my wife and I have received from working with the university students in the church we attend is that we've listened and we better understand the changes that are going on.

Bailey: Seasoned pastors need to develop relationships with younger pastors, rather than the usual top-down approach; likewise younger pastors need to be exposed to older pastors. Both need to adopt a posture that will be mutually beneficial. Just as older pastors have something to offer this younger generation, they too have something to offer to us.

Wiersbe: They help us catch up on the present!

Bailey: If you understand that, then in terms of what you have to offer, they will draw it out of you and ask for it, except you must give some level of respect to the values of their generation. Subsequently, they'll want to be close to you, and both of you will be helped. This will also prevent you from getting stale and staid. You won't be a relic of another age, and you can cross generations in your ministry. Artists in the music entertainment field do this, so why can't we do it? The preacher with the right attitude can transcend decades.

I'm in my midfifties, and my 11:00 A.M. worshipers' age range is eighteen to thirty-five. Well, it's not normal for a man in my age bracket to draw that kind of crowd, but there's a reason. I've taken several steps to demonstrate to them that I appreciate them, that I know where they are and what they're looking for. I appreciate their contribution to society today, and I understand their language. I don't try to be eighteen or thirty-five, but neither do I make myself superior to them. We all accept and appreciate each other.

Wiersbe: The worst thing we can do is to imitate them and pretend that we're something that we aren't and never can be. It's a two-way street; we accept them as they are and they accept us as we are, and we learn from and help each other.

Bailey: I let them know that I have studied and that I understand their values, as much as a man my age can. I let them know that I have values too. Some of our values are similar, but some of them are different. I make it a point to recognize and respect where they are, and they give me the same kind of respect. I use some of their vocabulary and jargon to let them know that, though I'm not one *of* them, I am one *with* them.

Wiersbe: We'd do the same thing if we were missionaries on a foreign field. I can't change my color or my ethnic background, but I can get acquainted with the language, mind-set, and culture of the people I'm trying to reach with the gospel. I can show respect for their heritage and use what I know to build bridges and not walls.

When a Sermon Bombs

How do you cope with discouragement when a sermon bombs? Are there specific steps we can take when we feel that a sermon missed the target? How do you overcome discouragement?

Wiersbe: Bailey's sermons never bomb.

Bailey: Yeah, right. Well, I think first and foremost you want to do a prayerful evaluation and be honest with yourself about your perceptions. Is it true that my sermon bombed? You can never really know that a sermon bombs, according to our definition, because many times when you think a sermon has bombed, it's been a blessing. If you can fish your ego out of the pond, then God does incredible things when you think you were not at your best. It's much like Paul's principle of "when I am weak, then I am strong." So when I think I've been very ineffective, I see that I've been strong because God has used my weakness to reveal himself to somebody in a way that I was not aware of at the time.

The other thing, of course, is that my wife has always been a pretty good gauge in my post-sermon evaluation. I remember something that happened thirty years ago. I preached on the text in Psalm 139: "Search me, O God, and know my heart." I knew the sermon was weak because I knew I hadn't put a lot of time in it. Once we were in the car, I was toying and fishing around for her comments. She said, "Bailey, that was the worst sermon I've ever heard you preach. You didn't spend any time studying, and it was obvious that you certainly had not spent much time with the Lord. You can preach better than that. And don't you ever go into the pulpit embarrassing God, me, or yourself like that again." And from that day to this one, I've had some other sermons that bombed, but she never had to say that to me again. She really made her point.

Wiersbe: Perhaps you heard about the pastor who preached what he thought was a great sermon and kept waiting for his wife to say something as they drove home. Well, she didn't say anything. He decided she just needed to be encouraged. So he said, "You know, there aren't many great preachers left in the world anymore." And she replied, "Yes, and there's one less than you think."

Bailey: Namely you.

Wiersbe: If you really want to get discouraged in preaching, preach in a radio studio. You have nobody responding. You don't hear laughter. You don't hear "Amen." You're just talking to a tape recorder or to an invisible congregation. And sometimes you wonder if you're sitting there talking to yourself. But years ago the Lord game me Jeremiah 1:12, "I am watching over my word to perform it." And I've held onto that. There are times I have slipped away from the pulpit knowing I could have done better, but also knowing that God promised to watch over his word and perform it. More than once, between my chair and the pulpit, I've sent up one of those Nehemiah prayers for help. "Lord, you know what this week has been like. I prepared the best I could. Help me!" And he'll say, "Let me take over, and we'll see what happens." And he does!

Bailey: Praise God, he does. Now, when I miss a week of preparation because of my own carelessness, it's unlikely that God will come through in that way. But when I miss a week because of legitimate interruptions, it's truly amazing what God will do with those kinds of experiences, just amazing.

Wiersbe: More than once, the Lord has awakened me in the night and given me the message. Right next to my bed, I keep a pad of paper and a pen with a light in it. When the Lord has awakened me and given me the message, I just write it down.

Spurgeon had an experience when he preached the sermon in his sleep. He had worked hard and couldn't get the message, and his wife told him to get some sleep and she'd wake him up early the next morning so he could work on the sermon. He started preaching and she wrote it down. The next morning she gave him the outline, and he said, "This is exactly what I want."

We will never know until we see Jesus whether the sermon was a bomb or a blessing. The messages that I think are gold, silver, and precious stones may turn out to be ashes, while a message I stumbled through may prove to be valuable in his sight. We preach by faith.

Bailey: One additional comment: there are some things we may know of that have precipitated the usurping of power and blessing while preaching. I think when it's obvious and we know it's not of God, then we're required to do something about it. When as much as you can tell you're moving in the same direction God is moving and the sermon still does not come across, I'm convinced that's when your faith kicks in and you leave it in God's hands.

When you're a pastor, you don't have time to wallow in despair and do a whole lot of regretting, because Sunday comes with such rapidity. You must get over those negative feelings and start up that hill again. The Bible says in Philippians 3:13: "One thing I do, forgetting those things which are behind and reaching forward to those things ahead."

Wiersbe: I think that we also need to live above impressions. Nothing can be more insidious than a religious feeling about something, because it could be the wrong thing. The Christian life is a life of obedience motivated by love. If in that pulpit we're obeying God, if it's the right message, with the right text, at the right time, and we want to glorify him, he's going to bless it ultimately. In John 6, Jesus preached away his whole congregation! I haven't done that yet. Our feelings are deceptive, and our evaluations can be wrong.

Bailey: What we're really talking about is the maturation process that must take place in the preacher, because most of us are not that mature. I'm not even sure if we ever get there, but it should be a goal that we set for ourselves. We should strive to take that attitude of faith, because the battle between Spirit and flesh is something we constantly deal with.

Wiersbe: I'm glad you brought that up, because there's a danger here of trying to become some kind of an icon. Some great preacher can get up and say very little, and people will swoon over it. I have the complete set of Spurgeon's printed sermons, and I've read some that were less than sensational. Even Babe Ruth didn't always hit home runs. We have to live above religious impressions. The same thing is true of personal witness. We have a minute or two to talk to somebody at the filling station, and we may wish we had done better, yet God will use that witness.

CHAPTER 4

THE DYNAMICS OF SERMON PREPARATION

*A*s discussed in the last chapter, personal preparation of the preacher's heart is critical to good preaching, whatever the ethnic setting. But as our conversation continues, the time has come to shift to the dynamics of preparing the sermon itself. So we begin by asking where good sermon ideas come from. What are some of the best places, best times, and best sources for sermon ideas?

Wiersbe: With me there's no one answer. A dedicated minister is always in a "preaching mode." We're constantly preparing, because the church and the messages are always on our heart. You're always thinking, praying, studying, keeping your eyes and ears open. Sometimes sermons come to me while I'm reading my Bible, and sometimes when I'm praying. I've even gotten ideas while shopping or looking for a parking place.

Bailey: Ideas and insights come from everywhere. A preacher can recognize preaching material anywhere if he is spiritually sensitive to God. All of life falls into one of two categories: it's either truth or error. Preaching does two things: it explains truth, and it exposes error. So you can preach on anything, because everything falls in one of those two categories. The Bible is our principal text and source for pulpit preaching, but the idea for the message can come out of *Time* magazine or it can come from watching a plane go across the sky. We relate everything to God and his Word.

Wiersbe: I get some of my best ideas from reading the newspaper, especially the comics. A good cartoonist sees life in a new light, and that shocks me out of my ruts. Humor has a way of helping us see another side of truth or error.

Bailey: Ideas certainly come from life experiences and from reading. This includes both secular and religious books. Creative people find sermon ideas in movies, television, family time, watching people, conversations, history, experiences, but most of all from the Bible.

Be Open to Life

Wiersbe: The preacher has to be open to life. Phillips Brooks said that ministry means higher heights of joy and deeper depths of sorrow. That doesn't mean we live on a roller coaster, because that would be neurotic. What he meant is that the preacher is experiencing great joy in one area of ministry while at the same time feeling great sorrow about some other area. These experiences help prepare our hearts to see God's truth.

But I've learned that after a period of intensive study, I have to get away from it for a short time and give the Lord opportunity to work it all into my mind and heart. I used to take Thursday as a day off, and almost every Thursday afternoon things would start to fall into place, and I'd go to my desk and finalize the message. Even while we're asleep, the Holy Spirit can work in our subconscious and teach us. More than once I've awakened in the morning and had the whole sermon development flash into my mind. One of my best sermons came to me while I was attending a funeral.

The mind grows by taking in, and the heart grows by giving out. I've learned that when I get out among the people—in the hospital or in the home—God talks to me about my sermons. I get back far more than I gave.

Bailey: This is true. The more we give out, the more the Lord sends back in.

How do you know what to preach on? How do you decide what's best out of all the ideas that come to you?

Bailey: Well, for me, there are two primary sources: the Word of God and the people. Preaching material comes strongly from both directions. The Word contains things that must be communicated on behalf of God, even though the people may not have a felt need. So you can't merely preach to meet felt needs, because the commandments of God need to be proclaimed regardless of the felt needs of the people. You'll never really know God if you don't use that approach. It is important to ask, What are the felt needs of the people? What do they sense that they need? I approach preaching both ways. I survey the congregation to find out their felt needs. I talk with people about what their deepest needs are. This gives me incredible information on what to preach. Then as I'm in my devotional time, I'm listening to what God has to say to me, and I am logging his directions away. It's sort of like breathing: there's a time to inhale and a time to exhale. So, determining what to preach, you have to look at both sides of that coin and avoid the rut of preaching only one side of it. You'll either miss God's message or miss the people's needs.

Wiersbe: That's pretty much my approach. On several occasions I have talked with the elders and asked for their guidance. I recall at Moody Church one summer when I was thinking about the fall preaching. I really didn't know what to preach. One of the elders spoke up and said, "Pastor, have you ever preached a series of sermons on suffering?" I never had. He said, "I think our people could use some messages on suffering." As I thought about it, I knew he was right, because many of our people were going through difficulties. Out of that suggestion came a series of messages as well as my book *Why Us? When Bad Things Happen to God's People.* When we're with our people, we need to take their pulse.

Sometimes we have to use the telescope and look ahead and prepare the church family for something that's coming. Correct me if I'm wrong in this, but I think God gives his servants a kind of spiritual radar that enables them to have an intimation that something is going to happen, and they want to prepare their people for it. We look into the Word, we look at the situations in people's lives, we look into our own hearts, and we look up for God's guidance. He has to put it all together.

Exegete the Culture

Bailey: Just let me add one other thing that we talked about earlier. African-American preachers would add that we need to exegete the culture and the times, along with exegeting the texts. You have to interpret what's going on in the larger society. If something happens that arrests the attention of the nation, state, or city, don't miss that opportunity to let God's Word speak to the situation.

I was in Oklahoma City the day the bomb went off. The explosion shook the hotel where I was staying and almost shook me out of bed. It was incredible to be in that city at that time. The church where I was preaching lost four members in that tragic event. Two of the members had been at church Monday night of the revival—the bomb went off on Tuesday—one was a deacon and the other was an usher. It was a moving experience to be with a church that was in pain and agony over what had happened.

The following Sunday I was preaching through Ephesians and had come to chapter 2. My congregation was somewhat removed from the bombing experience, but I delivered them to the scene and used that experience to introduce the chapter. They shared my experience of being there and being touched by what occurred. If something significant is going on in the nation, or even the city, I think we can either break into our series or, better yet, fit it into the sermon we've planned.

Wiersbe: I agree. But it's important that we don't preach the news story but rather the spiritual meaning in the story. As facts come out, stories change, so we have to be careful not to try to be amateur news analysts. But the eternal truths about man and God never change. Remember how Jesus dealt with the local tragedies the people asked him about (Luke 13:1–9). He made those stories personal and talked about repentance.

Plan Ahead

What about the whole area of planning ahead? If you plan ahead, is there a danger that you may lose some of the values of spontaneity in preaching?

Wiersbe: You plan ahead, but you don't finalize ahead. If I prepared a sermon four weeks in advance, I'd have to spend hours going through it again to be able to get warmed up to preach it. Now, that may just be a weakness on my part. You can plan ahead and even do exegesis in advance. You can make outlines. You can do all sorts of things in advance and put them in the file folder. But I have to finalize the next Sunday's message during that week before, or it will be a dud. The fire can get low in your soul. Without planning, you're drifting. But I don't think that a plan should be a straitjacket; I think it should be a compass.

Bailey: Both the pastor and the people get far much more out of the preaching when there is a preaching plan. Now, I consider my congregation a spontaneous people by and large, but I still plan, and I print the schedule in the bulletin so they know what's coming. I enjoy building the interest from one message to another.

Wiersbe: We have to create an appetite and then feed it. But preaching that's predictable isn't usually powerful, so we shouldn't tell them too much in advance, just enough to create that appetite.

Bailey: Each Sunday I give them two or three sentences about next Sunday's sermon, and they hang onto that. They bring their friends. "Guess what our pastor is going to be preaching about?" We even have little cards with the month's subjects printed on it, and I tell them to give them to their friends. They enjoy doing that. And if I announce that the Lord has laid another message on my heart, nobody is going to fall on the floor or call me in on the carpet. They want me to be a spokesman for God.

Wiersbe: They're going to listen more intently.

Bailey: They're going to listen to try to find out why the Lord changed the message. They want to hear God's Word. My people know that unless something really critical happens, I'm going to follow the announced schedule, because that's been my pattern all these years. But they also know that if I change the schedule, I've got a reason for it. I'm not just loafing.

Length of Sermon Preparation

What do you think is a reasonable amount of time to spend in preparation for sermons?

Wiersbe: As much as you can get. We must guard our preparation time jealously.

I'm up early each day, and when I was in the pastorate, I'd spend my mornings in study. But if you're preaching through a book of the Bible, there's no sense exegeting the three verses you're preaching about the next Sunday. Exegete an entire section of Scripture and work ahead. It will save you time. I think it's not a matter of budgeting time so much as prioritizing our time. If I have three hours at my disposal, I'm not going to answer mail or make a visit, unless it's an emergency. I'm going to work on the message.

Bailey: I think it's a personal matter, and in addition to what you just said, it's also a matter of experience. As a younger preacher, it took me a whole lot longer to put sermons together than it does now. A few years ago my wife observed that I didn't spend as much time in the study as I used to but that my preaching hadn't been affected. But after thirty-six years in the pulpit, I hope I know more than I used to know, and I know where to find what I need faster.

Wiersbe: Dr. Lloyd Perry used to tell us that the art of expository preaching is in knowing how to use the wastebasket, and he was right. You can't drop everything into one sermon. I have a friend who tries to say everything. Whatever is in the text, he's going to preach the whole thing. You can't do that—unless you want to sound like a commentary. In the first place, you don't know everything that's in the text or related to it. We have to focus our sermons and not try to hit every target. In these later years I'm seeing things come together in new ways. The other day it dawned upon me that I had given messages on three different texts that really belong together. Now three sermons can be developed into one message that says it better. I didn't see that ten years ago.

Bailey: Last week I announced what I was going to preach about, and Thursday night I thought the sermon preparation was over. I woke up Friday morning, looked at the outline, and the message didn't have any zip. And I said, "Is this what you're going to preach about on Sunday?" So between Friday and Saturday, I prepared a new sermon.

Wiersbe: I've been through that. But I'll tell you what's scary. It's happening to me these days, and I don't know why. Maybe it's also happened to you. Sometimes when I'm out in conference ministry, the message I want to preach doesn't really ignite until four or five hours before the meeting, and I don't know why. I'm the kind that wants to be ready well in advance, and sometimes the Lord keeps putting it off. He says, "Just trust me now. We're going to work this thing out. I can do it without you, but you can't do it without me. But trust me." It's testing my faith, believe me.

Study Resources

What resources have you found to be most helpful for sermon preparation?

Wiersbe: Anything other than homiletical commentaries that give you the sermon. Because if you read Maclaren or John Stott first, you're going to be tempted to preach them.

Bailey: If you read them prior to your own preparation, you're going to preach them.

Wiersbe: Right. I turn to their books after I've done my own outline.

Bailey: But if you do your exegesis and your own spadework, then you might find a critical line or a quote, which adds spice to your message. But if you read homiletical commentaries prior to your study, it will shape your thinking, and your creativity and uniqueness leap out the window. So I don't read sermon books until I have done what I'm supposed to do. Then in wrapping it up, maybe that second or third version, I'll go back and read the sermons of other preachers. If they have good quotes or an illustration or idea that will really add some zip to my message, then I take a look at it and maybe use it.

Wiersbe: That's pretty much my pattern.

Bailey: They call it looking at the lightweight, middleweight, and heavyweight commentaries.

Other than commentaries, are there any tools that you find helpful?

Wiersbe: One book that has been very helpful to me is *The Treasury of Scriptural Knowledge*. It contains half a million cross-references, covering almost every verse in the Bible. There's a new edition out now from Thomas Nelson. The Bible is its own best commentary, and I learn a lot by tracing the cross-references.

Bailey: I think that word studies are very important. I appreciate the books that help those of us who are not proficient in Greek and Hebrew. Knowing the rich meanings of Bible words makes a difference in our preaching. It's like watching color television instead of black and white. Words become pictures, and people don't easily forget a picture.

Sermon Introductions

What are some of the most important things about preaching you never learned in the classroom but learned only through experience?

Bailey: Well, for me, introductions are much more important and they need to have diversity. When I started preaching, my basic approach to introductions was to survey the biblical background. I would start out the sermon giving background of the text, and so every introduction became predictable. As I get older, I enjoy the people not knowing exactly what approach I will take, because I diversify the introduction from week to week. Last Sunday I went back to a biblical background approach, but I hadn't done that in months.

Wiersbe: So the old approach became new.

Bailey: It was fresh. It was new. The Sunday before that it was a laundry list of things. Before that it was a personal experience of someone else. It was a life-experience kind of thing. I enjoy starting sermons with illustrations, shocking statements, or powerful quotations because they really hook the people in the introduction. If you can get them on board, it's in the introduction that the preacher must touch on the text, the subject, and the congregation's interest, and you have to do that rather quickly. So when you diversify the introduction, then you get people locked in, even the ones who didn't come with a great desire to hear someone preach. The preacher must pull the congregation into that text by means of their experiences in life. If the introduction is creative and diversified and touches all those areas, there's a good chance that the people will give you a hearing. I didn't learn that in college and seminary. I learned that after graduation. The same thing applies to the sermon's conclusion. Strive for variety.

Wiersbe: When I was in seminary in the late forties, classic homiletics was starting to move off the scene, and preachers were discovering imagination. The classic sermon opened with a review of the setting of the text, then moved into a statement that announced the theme and approach. The outline was supposed to help explain and apply the passage. Like you, I've changed my approach to introductions and to sermon structure in general. I like to start way out in left field, get their attention and interest, and then pull them into the text. And the more familiar the text is, the more you've got to start out in left field. If you're going to preach on the Twenty-third Psalm, you had better begin somewhere else, because everybody thinks they know Psalm 23. They've heard it at a hundred funerals.

Bailey: I was just now thinking about your homiletical approach to Psalm 23 and how you named all those animals.

Wiersbe: I try to hit the pulpit running. When you're preaching for eternity, time is precious, and we can't afford to waste it chatting about the weather. Another thing I've changed is in making the application. We were taught to preach the text and conclude with the application. But the way to do it is the way Jesus did it: apply the truth throughout the message. The Holy Spirit is applying the truth to hearts as we preach, and so should we.

I've also taken a new approach to illustrations. We were told to use illustrations like condiments, dropping them into the message to make it more palatable—here a story, there a poem, here another story. Today I don't do that. If I'm trying to make something clear or drive something home to the heart, I use an illustration. Sometimes I use illustrations to stimulate their attention, especially when I've been dealing with something difficult. But if my explanation has been clear, why should I have to illustrate it? I make an exception only when the story is so great, you can't afford not to use it.

CHAPTER 5

THE DYNAMICS OF SERMON CONTENT

Most people who slip into a pew on Sunday don't have a clue how much work has taken place behind the scenes to prepare for the sermon. But as E. K. Bailey and Warren Wiersbe talk, we begin to catch a glimpse of their diligent work behind the scenes—work that's hidden from the average service attender. Anyone who has ever prepared to preach a sermon, however, will be able to identify with some of the issues that emerge in the conversation. So let's listen in and see what we can learn.

> *How do you go about creating and constructing a sermon? Do you put an outline together? Do you jot down notes, or do you write out a full manuscript?*

Wiersbe: The structure of the sermon depends a good deal on the text and on what you want the sermon to accomplish. You don't treat Psalm 23 the way you do Romans 4. It depends on the kind of biblical literature that you're dealing with. It also depends on the congregation, the purpose of the message, and what the text says. So the actual structure has to grow out of the living dynamics between the preacher's heart and mind, the congregation, and the text. Otherwise, every week the sermon structure will be the same. The Bible gives us infinite variety—poetry, narrative, didactic teaching, even riddles. Sameness leads to tameness.

I've not been in the habit of manuscripting my messages. I don't know when I would have had time to do it. But I think them through and try to incarnate them. I make an outline, and I take the outline with me, but I try not to depend on it. However, at this stage in life, I don't want to take chances. I think our final message also depends on the inspiration of the moment. There are things that God does during the preaching event that amaze us.

That creative moment of delivery is crucial?

Wiersbe: I guess that depends on the Holy Spirit and what they call "unction." One preacher said, "I don't know what unction is, but I know when it isn't there!" I mull over the text. I pray. I meditate and exegete. I talk to my Bible and ask questions of the text. I take notes. I think. I sweat. And then God gives me what he wants me to have. Often while I'm preaching, I say things spontaneously that amaze me and everybody else. It's not direct inspiration, obviously; it's more like illumination, and the light comes on brighter.

Jewel, Twin, and Telescope Sermons

Bailey: Well, I fully agree. It was Dr. Caesar Clark who told me in my early pastoring days, "Son, always go with the grain of the text." It certainly all depends on the text, because a right understanding of the text will dictate the structure, direction, and flow of the sermon. I also try to bring a creative flair and "antennae" to the sermon preparation, because even if you choose a text similar to other texts, you can still make sure that the approach to the text is different.

For instance, I sometimes preach what I call a jewel sermon. I take the text and turn it around and look at the many facets. I take a line, a phrase, a word, and turn it around and around, and everything I say is emanating from that particular part of the text. I could do an exposition of three or four lines or the entire passage, but in this particular case, for variety's sake, I do a jewel sermon based on the passage.

Or we might do a twin sermon, where one line deals with the negative aspect of an issue and the next line the positive. There are only two points: what should not be done versus what should be done, a lie versus the truth. And you just parallel those two aspects as you work through the text. You can still bring variety to preaching, but at the same time, you're being consistent and accurately interpreting the text. So I agree with what you said. First and foremost, the sermon is based on what the text has to say. The challenge is to add diversity to your approach in opening up that text.

Wiersbe: One of my favorite sermon structures is the telescope sermon, where each point comes out of the previous point. I have a sermon on John 15—"Five Secrets of Living"—that takes this approach. Here's the outline:

1. The secret of living is fruit-bearing
2. The secret of fruit-bearing is abiding in Christ
3. The secret of abiding is obeying
4. The secret of obeying is loving
5. The secret of loving is knowing Christ better

Each successive point grows out of the preceding point, like pulling out the segments of a telescope.

Expository Sermons

What do you think about expository preaching versus topical preaching and other approaches? You talked about the jewel sermon, the twin sermon, and the telescope sermon. Do you believe in the expository method? Is that the best method? Or has the time for expository preaching passed, and should we be moving on to greater variety?

Wiersbe: All biblical preaching is exposition—explaining and applying God's truth. An expository sermon is the explanation and application of a portion of Scripture in an organized manner. That's all it is. You can expound a word, a theme, a verse, a chapter, even an entire book of the Bible. So from my viewpoint, all biblical preaching is expository.

Bailey: Yes, I agree. But it has to be more than just a verse-by-verse commentary. That's called a running commentary.

Wiersbe: You're talking about expository preaching after the manner of Martyn Lloyd-Jones. In his Friday evening Bible school he spent fourteen years expounding the epistle to the Romans. I'm afraid the attention span of the average person today isn't what it was back in those days, and Lloyd-Jones was a uniquely gifted preacher of incredible stature in the Christian world. I think you can do thematic preaching by choosing a Bible passage that focuses on that theme and expounding it. But the word-by-word, verse-by-verse approach isn't as popular as once it was. If the preacher works hard at variety, he can do it.

Bailey: People today expect variety. They get it everywhere else, why not from the pulpit?

Wiersbe: Sameness of approach and sermon structure may mean we're ignoring the congregation and its needs. The message must be prepared for the people. If we can preach the same sermon in ten other places without making some changes in it, there's something wrong with the sermon. It's generic, and generic sermons don't move people's hearts. I think that good exposition has the needs of the people in mind.

Bailey: Absolutely, and even exposition must have variety. You can do an exposition of one word, a phrase, a whole passage, and you can do an exposition of a theme. In topical exposition you look at the felt needs of people, but you're answering those needs by the exposition and application of the Word of God. That's where a lot of my preaching seems to be moving these days. I still do classic exposition of particular passages, but I'm doing much more topical exposition where I address an issue from a biblical point of view. I may have a principal text, but I'm mobilizing the totality of the truth of the Word of God behind that particular idea and letting people see that this is a Scripture-wide issue rather than something that's isolated in one particular verse, chapter, or book of the Bible. Different verses will give different slants on the same truth, and so I try to address the issue from various viewpoints.

In the African-American church today, what would be the most common style of preaching? Is your approach atypical, or are there others who preach with the same approach?

Bailey: I don't think that my approach is atypical. Much of our African-American preaching is still topical preaching, but I see the beginning of a paradigm shift, maybe over the last ten years or so. God has increased and elevated many expositors in the African-American community. As he does in his inimitable way, he has sovereignly selected some of the most influential preachers in our culture and turned them toward expository preaching. As a result, their influence has really persuaded large numbers of African-American preachers to move into expository preaching. I see a swelling of interest in exposition around the country, especially in the young preachers.

Can you give an example from your annual conferences on expository preaching?

Bailey: Yes. We invite some of the top expositors from across the country, both African-Americans and Caucasian, because we want to cross-pollinate and learn from one another. But we always invite some younger pastors to preach. I want the conferees to know that you don't have to be fifty years old before you're invited to participate on a national platform. We are seeing in these young preachers some tremendous gifts for doing expository preaching. But I think this whole idea of topical exposition is something that shouldn't be ignored. I was introduced to the concept only a few years ago, and I really had a hard time breaking away from my training in majoring on expository preaching. So I came home and tried it, and the congregational response to it was just incredible, and that's really what convinced me that I was onto something. I'm not seeing a lot of it across the country as of yet, but there are a few who have been introduced to the idea of topical exposition. But with the younger generation, I'm seeing that they are very, very interested and that they have embraced the concept of topical exposition.

Wiersbe: I was just running through in my mind some of the preachers I've read over the years and the approaches they took. George W. Truett frequently did what you just described. He'd read the text, choose a topic from the text, and preach the topic biblically. He was not a traditional expositor. He would pull from the text a spiritual principle—a topic, if you please—and then explain and apply the principle. Spurgeon took a similar approach and occasionally used the text more like a motto. But he was always teaching the truth of the Word of God. You use a text as a motto when you ignore the context. I think the key issue is balance. It's just like eating meals at home. Spinach is good for me, but if I had spinach three times a day, seven days a week, I'd get tired of it. Variety is very important.

Spurgeon told about two farmers who met at the market one Monday morning and got to chatting about church the day before. "What did your minister preach?" asked one man, and his friend replied, "Oh, the same old thing—ding-dong, ding-dong, ding-dong." The other farmer said, "You should be thankful! All we hear is ding, ding, ding, ding."

Scripture as the Foundation

Should Scripture always serve as the foundation for every sermon? Why?

Wiersbe: Well, it's the only authority we have for life and godliness. Who am I that I should tell people about God without some authority backing up my words? The preaching of the Word is what God has used to get his work done on earth. When Paul said to "preach the word," he didn't mean "preach about the word."

I won't mention his name, but many years ago there was a famous American evangelist about the same time that Billy Graham's ministry was on the rise. This evangelist drew bigger crowds and got better reviews than Graham did. Then he moved off the scene and finally left the ministry completely. One day I took a couple of his books off the shelf and read the sermons. The titles were clever; they got your attention. The introductions grabbed you. But the sermons contained very little biblical truth or even quotations from Scripture. They were skyscraper sermons—one story on top of another. The preacher needs the Bible for his own spiritual nourishment and guidance. If I get away from the Word of God in my preaching and my writing, my ministry has ceased. The Word of God endures. My clever ideas won't last.

Bailey: God's Word is central. It is our only authority. How we come to that authority in our preaching may vary. Historically, we have started with the Bible, and then what we say springs from the text. In terms of preaching to today's younger generation, it's sometimes necessary to identify spiritual problems that they consistently encounter and their legitimate spiritual needs and then search and examine the Scriptures for the biblical approach and mandate regarding these problems. Many times I have started with the application as an attention getter and then worked my way back to the central truth.

Wiersbe: And defended it.

Bailey: Yes. This generation is asking, "What's in it for me?" It demands better preaching and more skillful preparation if we're going to get through to their minds and hearts. If they possess a "consumer mentality," then we don't do any injury to the gospel by inverting our approach and starting where they are and then back them into the truth and the authority of the Word of God. When it comes to this younger generation, I often ask, "Did you know that God said this thousands of years ago?" The majority of them are astonished that the Bible addresses so many contemporary ideas. So you can come to the Word from different directions and reach this generation.

Wiersbe: The major image of the church today seems to be the shopping mall: here's something for everybody, and parking must be close to the front door. If you don't want to come to Sunday school, but you want to be part of a music group, that's fine. I once heard Stuart Briscoe say that every local church must have many doors through which people can enter. We had people come to Moody Church for the music who didn't care much about my preaching. You get them in and then you go after them. I think preachers can learn from the commercial paradigm. Do my sermons have something for everybody? Of course, the gospel and Jesus Christ meet the needs of everybody, but I'm talking about the packaging of the truth, the approach. If you'll excuse the term, I'm referring to the "selling" of the product.

How do older folks like my wife and I shop? Suppose we need a new dishwasher. The first thing my wife does is talk to her friends and ask what kind of dishwashers they have and how they like them. Then she watches the newspaper and magazine ads. Then she goes to her favorite appliance store and looks over their wares and asks questions. She waits and takes time to digest all these experiences. Finally she goes and buys the one she wants. Today's young people don't follow that approach. That's not the way they operate. They might check the marketing channels on television—

Bailey: They go online and let the computer do the shopping.

Wiersbe: Exactly. Our older daughter spends time on the computer and finds all kinds of bargains. In preaching to the younger generations, we will have to deal more with options: this is what the world offers, this is what you want, this is what the Lord offers you. It's the parable of the prodigal son all over again. The boy had several options and made the wrong choices based on the wrong values.

The consumer mentality of today's worshiper—what you call "What's in it for me?"—gives us a creative metaphor for preaching. You take what you want from life, but you eventually pay for it. The message of the gospel offers no bargains. Salvation cost Jesus his life, and it costs us something to receive Christ and follow him.

Changes in Approach

Both of you have mentioned changes you've made in your approach to preaching. Anything more you'd like to add?

Wiersbe: I used to think that everything in the sermon had to be alliterated. Several of the preachers I admired when I was young always followed that pattern. I've moved away from that. Now I alliterate only if it comes naturally and helps the sermon. Lloyd Perry, who taught me in seminary, would say to us, "Gentlemen, remember, alliteration will sell you short every time." And it will!

A shorter introduction is another change I've made, plus applying the Word as I go along. I use more narrative bridges, so that the sermon is a seamless robe rather than a patchwork quilt. The biggest change in my preaching style and approach has been release from standing behind the pulpit. At Moody Church, you couldn't step out of the pulpit, you'd have broken a leg. I move around on the platform now and have even been known to leave the platform. Today's media generation is accustomed to watching change and movement. On MTV the picture never stands still, and in most TV programs the bytes are about forty-five seconds long. The preacher today needs to modulate his voice and change his position on the platform. We must use meaningful gestures, otherwise we lose their attention. Another change is not being so content-centered. There's still content—I still teach the Bible—but now I focus more on intent. I keep my eyes on the goal.

Bailey: I want to piggyback on that. For many years my tradition as well as my temperament kept me behind the pulpit. But in recent years, after reading, studying, and attempting to reach out to the younger generations, I found that it was very important to be released from the pulpit. I also discovered that the pulpit was an obstruction for many of the listeners. This generation is very skeptical of authority and authority figures. What they really want to know is, "Are you for real?" They've seen so much hypocrisy and duplicity in our day that when something stands between you and them, you send the wrong message. They want to be able to have more of an intimate relationship with the person who's speaking, without any obstruction between the two, and being free helps me make a vital connection with the people. A woman phoned and told me she really enjoyed the sermon, but even more, she enjoyed the approach and the delivery. She felt connected to the person who was communicating the Word.

Wiersbe: In some churches the pastor is a worshiper sitting in the third row and doesn't get up on the platform until he preaches. In other words, not only is the pulpit out of the way, but the platform is out of the way. When the minister steps up to preach, he's one of the worshipers. In the church we attend, all we have on the platform is the worship team, the musicians, and the instruments. The pastor sits with the congregation on the right-hand side in the third row. We know he's there. When visitors come in, they wonder who is going to preach. Then he gets up and preaches. They like that. The older folks had to get used to this. The pastor took all the chairs off the platform, and now nobody sits in Moses' seat.

Bailey: Well, at our church, we do the chairs-and-pulpit thing at the 8:00 A.M. service, but it's all removed at our 11:00 A.M. service. Because we're trying to adapt to the mind-set of this younger generation, we have a team of men who work between the services to clear the platform. At our 8:00 A.M. service, the worshipers are looking for that icon, they look for that father figure, and they look for that shepherd. This younger generation doesn't really look for that; in fact, it turns them off. I had to get used to that myself.

Wiersbe: Do you change clothes between services?

Bailey: Sometimes.

Wiersbe: I have no problem with *adapting* the ministry to the people we're trying to reach, but when we start *accommodating,* we must be cautious. In 1 Thessalonians 2:3, Paul said, "For our exhortation did not come from deceit or uncleanness, nor was it in guile." In verse 5 he added, "For neither at any time did we use flattering words." Once we start to accommodate our ministry and message just to please people, we've given up authentic ministry.

Bailey: Oh yes, and I'm keenly aware of the difference. In 1 Corinthians 9:22, Paul said, "I become all things to all men so that I might win some." I think that adapting has to do with the methods. But the message is eternal, and that we never change.

Wiersbe: It's possible to have a seeker-friendly church and still not compromise. I preached in a church in California where thousands of people attended three services on a Sunday morning. Every generation and social level was represented in each congregation. They sang songs about the blood of Christ and even sang some hymns. It was almost like a traditional service, but the atmosphere was not traditional, and the pastor's handling of the platform was not traditional. But I know of some seeker-sensitive churches that have banned songs about the blood lest they "offend" the lost people present.

Windows on the Word

What's the role of illustrations? How do you find them? How do you use illustrations effectively?

Bailey: Well, I enjoy finding and using illustrations. It was Spurgeon who said that illustrations are windows to the sermon and should let in the light. Illustrations are critical because they help us explain and enforce the truth of the text. An illustration is like a story. People remember stories, and when they do, they'll also remember the principle or lesson behind the story. In fact, they will back their way through the illustration to the principle. So I think it's very important that you do have illustrations, because that's how people can identify with what you're preaching about.

Where do you find them? If your eyes are open and your spiritual antenna is up, you find them everywhere. First of all, I think biblical illustrations are the best, because they have the authority of the Lord behind them. As a preacher does his daily devotions, as he reads and studies the Bible, he sees illustrations of biblical truth. I literally page through the Scripture, or I go through the Scripture in my mind, trying to find that event or person that illustrates the point of the text. Then I'll do some strong research to make sure I'm interpreting the material correctly and contextually.

When it comes to personal illustrations, they can be very effective; however, we must be careful not to portray ourselves as the hero all of the time. Let me caution the younger preachers to have a balance, so that sometimes you come out the hero and sometimes you come out the goat. People need to know that I'm not Jesus' brother. I'm pursuing the same type of righteousness that they are pursuing, and I share the same struggles. So don't be the hero who has always done everything right. The people know better. Illustrate where you made mistakes, where you had a misconception about things, and how God helped you to overcome. I like to use real-life illustrations that come from the experiences of other people. If an illustration involves your family or someone in the church, please ask their permission before using it.

I love reading biographies and autobiographies. There is so much illustrative material found in the lives of men and women, both past and present, who have achieved and accomplished great things. What I am looking for are glimpses of how God worked in their lives, so I can incorporate those truths into my own life in order to share them with other people. You will also find a plethora of illustrations through reading magazines and good newspaper articles if you can't afford the time to read biographies. You can also use your imagination and create your own illustrations, comparable to the way Jesus spoke in parables. I enjoy telling stories I have made up. Those listening are not aware it's a story until you tell them. Even though it clarifies the point, you must maintain your integrity by briefly explaining that the story was something from your creative imagination. You can easily do that before you transition into the text or an application. These are just some of the ways I find illustrations. I don't get many illustrations out of illustration books.

Wiersbe: I usually tell my students to stay away from illustration books. Most of the illustrations in them are quite old and threadbare, and there are a lot of errors passed from one book to another. They print stories about events that never happened. Have you seen the book *They Never Said It?* It's a secular book about things great people never said but that are frequently attributed to them. This happens in illustration books. The only thing we have to watch out for when it comes to personal illustrations is to get permission if we ever involve our family members in a story, especially the children. They should know we're going to do it. Our kids don't like to be embarrassed from the pulpit.

Bailey: I learned that the hard way.

Wiersbe: We all did, brother. The second thing is not to shoot from the hip. To pull an unprepared illustration out of thin air may work, but it may not. It may embarrass you. I have to resist that sometimes. I'm better at remembering quotations than I am at recalling stories. You know, this business of using Bible illustrations is a wonderful way to teach new Christians how practical the Bible is.

Years ago Dr. Roy Laurin wrote a book called *Meet Yourself in the Bible.* It's now out of print. You can actually meet yourself in the Bible. When you use Bible illustrations, you're saying to people that God's Word is about you and me today, not only about people in ancient history. The worst illustration is the one that comes out of a book and is about people nobody knows and events that nobody understands.

Dr. Louis Paul Lehman was a master sermon illustrator. At breakfast once, I saw him pick up four or five wrapped soda crackers and put them in his pocket. That evening as he was preaching, he took them out of his pocket and just held them and talked about the need for unity among God's people. He put all the crackers on top of each other and said, "This isn't unity; it's uniformity. I'll show you unity." He took all the crackers out of their wrappers and smashed them together. "Do you know why we don't have unity? We're not broken." I don't recall what he said in the rest of the sermon, but I can't forget that illustration.

Bailey: When an illustration leans toward the incredible, you need to verify the illustration's legitimacy by giving one or two words of factual background. We frequently hear about the man who walked across Niagara Falls on a high wire. If we're going to use that story, we'd better know his name, when the event took place, and who recorded it. It is important to provide names, dates, and relevant facts that lend to the illustration's credibility. Then people can go verify the story if they want to. The story may have sounded incredible, but it's verifiable.

Wiersbe: Credibility comes from facts and documentation. If a speaker introduces a quotation with, "One of our presidents said . . . ," it doesn't mean very much. But if the preacher says, "In his first inaugural address, given on March 4th, 1933, President Franklin Delano Roosevelt said, 'We have nothing to fear but fear itself,'" he's given authenticity to the quotation. Most scholarly quotation books, like the *Oxford Book of Quotations,* will usually provide documentation.

Narrative Preaching and Preaching Narrative

How should narrative and storytelling be used in sermons? Do you have any cautions, guidelines, or examples?

Wiersbe: I think all good preaching is storytelling in one way or another. If a story means we've got a plot—we're starting here and we're ending there—that's what good preaching is. There's a difference between preaching narrative and narrative preaching. You can preach Bible narrative in outlined sermonic form. But in narrative preaching, we jump into the "story river" and it carries us along. The danger of narrative preaching is the minimizing of theology and the maximizing of imagination. Just telling the story isn't the same as preaching the message of the story. We end up entertaining rather than edifying. If in telling the story we would do what Jesus did and reveal truth about God and man, then wrap the whole thing up with a challenge, we'd accomplish more. Narrative preaching is difficult to do, but it's rewarding. I've never done "personality preaching," where you impersonate a Bible character. It too has its dangers.

Bailey: I've done narrative preaching, and I love it. Dr. Henry Mitchell says that a tale well told not only appeals to the intellect but also sets a fire of emotional joy.

What about using narrative in different parts of the sermon, but not the whole sermon?

Wiersbe: In some sermons I have carried on imaginary conversations with Bible characters, and it's worked well. But I doubt that I could sustain that approach for an entire sermon. I'd probably stop preaching and start acting!

Bailey: One of the creative things about preaching is to change the approach from point to point just for variety and emphasis. I may do straight exposition on point one, but point two may be a narrative approach. So not only do I move to a different point in the message, but I also move to a different style of preaching, and this seizes and holds the attention of the people.

Wiersbe: That's excellent, but it takes experience to be able to shift the gears while the car is racing down the highway!

Bailey: It's worth the effort. October was Women's Month at our church, and I preached on different women in the Bible.

Wiersbe: The bad girls of the Bible?

Bailey: The bad girls of the Bible and some of the best girls I have read about. One of the bad girls who became a good girl was Rahab. Well, during the introduction and the first point, I took a traditional approach to the Scripture. The second point was narrative style, and I focused on what was going on between Rahab and the spies. The people really got caught up in that particular part of the sermon. This approach isn't unique to African-American preachers. For African-American preachers, the whole idea of storytelling started with the fact that our people have depended on stories and oral tradition, even from our African days. Before we became a literate people, our history was passed down through oral communication.

So the art of telling stories has been a cultural treasure, helping to keep our history alive. This storytelling art was translated over into our preaching, and I hope we never lose it. When an African-American church wants to get an evaluation of a preacher, one important question they ask is, "Can he tell the story?"

Wiersbe: But some preachers can't tell the story and get the message across. They just retell a Bible story and call it a sermon. Another approach to narrative preaching is to interview a Bible character at some point in the message. You're preaching from John 3 about the new birth, and you carry on a conversation with Nicodemus. You ask the questions the people in the congregation are asking in their own minds, and Nicodemus answers them.

What about the related trend in recent years of using drama before or after the message? Sometimes the drama is dropped into the middle of the sermon. What's the relationship between drama and preaching?

Bailey: I've used drama as my sermon introduction. The drama team did the introduction, and I immediately entered the pulpit after their presentation and preached. Pow! I transitioned right into the sermon. I've had people give testimonies in the middle of the sermon, and I've also inserted a skit or two into the sermon. I've also used movie clips in the sermon. Recently my wife spoke at the church for Women's Day and used a clip of Whoopi Goldberg from *Sister Act II*. Well, that was her introduction. There was a song entitled "Sister's in Trouble," and it arrested the attention of the congregation because everybody was familiar with it. So we integrate drama and technology to communicate the message. You have to be careful, because you can overdo anything good. However, if the film clip is timely and consistent with what you're talking about, by all means, go ahead and use it. If it's just something off in left field, it will ruin everything. It must be consistent with the theme of the message and not a distraction.

Wiersbe: My only concern about film clips is that we don't give the impression that we're approving the entire film just because we excerpt a tiny part. We might inadvertently create a problem for some parents. Some of the most refreshing preaching I have personally done has followed a good drama.

I was at the College Church in Wheaton, Illinois, for their Summerfest, and I spoke every night on one of the parables. They had assigned this to me, and they had written a drama to go with each message. Each night I just stepped up after the drama and started preaching, and the crowd was really ready.

The Bible is a book of drama. You find a number of dramas that I call "action sermons," such as Jeremiah at the potter's house breaking a jar (Jeremiah 19). That's an action sermon. The book of Ezekiel records many action sermons. In Ezekiel 4, the prophet had to "play war" and portray the fall of Jerusalem. Then he had to lie on his left side a certain number of days and on his right side for another number of days. God told Ezekiel to dig through the wall like an escaping prisoner of war. His neighbors saw all this and wondered what he was doing, and this paved the way for the preaching of the Word. I have no problem with drama provided the tail doesn't wag the dog. I was at a service where most of the crowd was under forty. The preacher was telling about our Lord's healing of a blind man, and at that point they showed a clip from the *Jesus* film of Jesus healing a blind man. It was powerful. He could have given an altar call right then.

Bailey: I agree with your concern about seeming to promote a movie rated beyond PG that is anti-Christian in its message. But I do think we can use these methods to help in communicating the gospel, which is our task. I think one of the dangers is that you can overdo it. I wouldn't do this every Sunday. I try to do these things on the "high days" of the calendar, such as Easter, Thanksgiving, and Christmas, when many visitors are present and our people think they've heard all there is to hear about those special days.

If I'm planning a dramatic-type sermon, I'll start announcing it a month in advance. I'll tell them that we're going to have a visitor from the first century, and everybody wonders what I'm talking about. One of the most exciting sermons was on Hosea, and then another one was about the confessions of an ex-crossmaker. When the people got here, they saw a workshop on the platform with saws and sawdust, and half-made crosses. When I came out I had on my carpenter's apron. Another sermon was Herod coming from hell, who told us what he did that sent him there. This was actually a whole production with other people involved in the presentation, and I had the lead part. It was an exciting drama. I like to do that kind of preaching for those high days when people expect a traditional sermon.

Social Issues in the Pulpit

What about addressing social issues from the pulpit?

Wiersbe: Man, if preaching isn't social, what is it?

Liberals preach on social issues, fundamentalists avoid them, and most evangelicals wrestle with them.

Bailey: Whites avoid it, and blacks sometimes overdo it. If you don't present the whole gospel for the whole person, then you're one-sided. Truth out of context and truth separated from other truths will lead to distortion, heresy, and worse, irrelevancy.

Mary and Martha were one-sided, and they each needed what the other one had. Martha is in the kitchen working, doing practical things, and is representative of the social-action side of the faith, while Mary is sitting at the feet of Jesus, listening to the Word—the worship side of the faith. The idea is to bring those two sisters together and let them cross-pollinate and learn from one another. There is that personal, evangelical, intimate side of your relationship with God, that you must be saved, sanctified, filled with the Spirit, walking in the fullness of Christ—all of these things are critical. But if all this wonderful experience doesn't bleed over into healing the hurts of humanity and bringing hope to the helpless, then we're not fully following Jesus.

Somewhere between two and three hundred Scriptures in the Bible speak about helping the poor, being concerned about bringing relief to those who are voiceless, disenfranchised, and left out. We need to provide resources for personal development so that people can stand on their own without having to be on welfare. Christians should be speaking to these issues and seeing what can be done about changing social and political structures so that people of all ethnic backgrounds can have equal access to the system. The key is access. Understanding that sin is both institutional as well as personal, how can we have access to the system and access to the American dream? Now, it's imperative to address social issues for those things to come to pass, understanding that sin is both institutional as well as personal. "All that is required for evil to triumph is for good men to do nothing."

Wiersbe: Agreed. But we are handicapped in the white church. If I preached Jesus' first sermon (Luke 4:14–30) and gave to it the social emphasis that he gave, our church has no vehicle for doing anything about the problem. People would respond in one of two ways: (1) "This preacher is off-base, so let's get rid of him," or (2) "I've never seen it quite that way, but what do I do next?" For the most part, our white churches don't have the instruments, the organizational structure, to get involved in social action. Our usual solution is to put some inner-city organization into the budget or maybe to collect and distribute used clothing. To many people, dealing with social problems ultimately means getting involved in politics, and politics and Christianity aren't supposed to mix.

When it comes to racial issues, many white churches will participate in any number of symbolic activities, but they're hesitant when you ask them to get involved in sacrificial services in the trenches. They would listen to E. K. Bailey preach and tell us what we should be doing, and would probably agree with E. K., but that may be as far as they will go.

Bailey: I've been meeting regularly with some white believers, hoping to encourage mutual concern and understanding.

It takes time; it isn't something that you push. What I really see is that the people don't have a clue as to what needs to be done. One of them said last time we met, "I've always wanted to ask African-Americans these questions, but I never knew one well enough that I felt comfortable asking." We were in the group one-and-a-half years, and this was the first time they'd dared to ask about critical issues! So it took that bonding time where they didn't think I was going to jump up and lash out at someone verbally, physically, or any other way. They finally felt comfortable enough to ask me tough questions and get answers from a man who loves Jesus.

Special Days and Seasons

What are some of the special days or seasons that are important to your community, and how do they influence your preaching?

Bailey: First and foremost is Martin Luther King's birthday in January, and something special is usually done in most African-American churches. At the Concord Church, we've had our speech choir, which is our children's choir, recite the "I Have a Dream" message, or the Gettysburg address, or something similar. The drama team may do something. And the sermon may be along the line of "The Dream Goes On" and give a modern-day interpretation of what that means for the dream to continue. That has influenced our worship services as well as our preaching, on a regular basis.

Many churches get together to celebrate. I was in Indianapolis on King Day, and over fifty churches came together in a mass service. That's being done annually all around the country, including in Dallas. Normally, if I'm not asked to speak, I will be at that service, and of course, we're usually encouraged as Christians to keep the dream alive, continue to fight for equality and access to the American dream.

Here in Texas, "Juneteenth" is still important. Juneteenth is the nineteenth of June and commemorates when the slaves heard they were free. That was two years after the

Emancipation Proclamation. Many times the celebration rolls over into the church, because that's a historical event that's really not celebrated outside of Texas. But in Texas, it is big.

Of course, on the larger calendar, Mother's Day and Father's Day are very important, and so is Thanksgiving Day, which is both civil and religious in nature. On the Christian calendar we have Easter and Christmas. But King Day and Juneteenth are the two days that make us focus primarily on our own heritage.

So you would interrupt any sermon series to commemorate those days?

Bailey: Knowing that they're coming, you could easily contextualize them and not interrupt the series. In fact, on King weekend I'm preaching on "Breaking the Cycle of Generational Curses." Well, African-Americans have a lot of generational curses that need to be broken. The sermon theme fits right in.

Wiersbe: White churches have these curses too, but we prefer to hide them.

Bailey: All of us are guilty of sin. Every family has iniquities that come down through the genes. But my people have to deal with some things that are uniquely ours because of the social situation, like black-on-black crime and family violence. Those kinds of things are somewhat unique to African-Americans. I need to tell them that Jesus can break this generational bondage and give them a new start in life.

The conversation on the content of sermons could have continued for some time. But it was time to take a break and digest what we had been discussing. Having covered preachers' personal preparation as well as preparation of the sermon, we still needed to focus on sermon delivery, giving special consideration to the differences that exist between black and white churches. To that subject we turn in the next chapter.

CHAPTER 6

THE DYNAMICS OF
SERMON DELIVERY

*S*uppose you attended a worship service in an African-American church
*in Birmingham or Boston, in Chattanooga or Chicago, then the fol-
lowing Sunday you attended a service in a predominantly Caucasian
congregation, and you were asked to describe the styles of sermon delivery.
Or suppose you were visiting in a city away from your home. So you turned
on the television in the hotel room where you were staying and caught a
half hour of a white service followed by a black service. What differences
might you see? How might the styles of sermon delivery differ? It has been
said, "Black preaching is a dialogue that does not occur after but during the
sermon. It is a call-and-response style of communication coming out of the
African tradition. The congregation is encouraged and expected to participate
in the act and art of preaching with verbal and body response."[4] Is that an
accurate characterization, or a stereotypical generalization?*

*Sitting in the lounge of the Concord Missionary Baptist Church in Dal-
las, we asked the senior pastor, What's unique about sermon delivery in the
black community as compared to the white community?*

Bailey: I think there are similarities and differences. I think that
all effective preaching tries to internalize the text to the
point that when it is preached, the listener experiences

---

[4]William Bailey McClain, "African-American Preaching," quoted in *Leadership
Handbooks of Practical Theology,* vol. 1, *Word and Worship,* ed. James D. Berkley
(Grand Rapids: Baker, 1992), 76.

the text. In his book *Celebration and Experience in Preaching,* Dr. Henry Mitchell says that the preacher's task is to provide a total experience of the gospel. The experience-centered gospel stimulates the growth of gut-level trust in God by providing involvement and encounters where faith had and has been caught and taught. Black preachers want to get into the text and feel it, touch it, taste it, smell it, rub shoulders with it, and then allow the people to experience the truth of the text.

Wiersbe: I think anything unique anywhere depends on the preacher and the church. The black community may be a different context altogether, because the congregation is an important part of the preaching. But too often we preachers in the white churches preach the way they expect us to preach. If I go to Third Reformed Church to speak, I probably wouldn't preach the way I would at Concord Church. Is there a consistent delivery from church to church in the black community? I didn't think so.

Bailey: No, it depends on the church and the pastor. People gravitate to the church and the preacher that best fit their values, expectations, or comfort zones.

Is there anything unique about the approach to sermon delivery?

Bailey: I think that in the African-American churches, the preacher has much more freedom. We are freer in what we can do and what we can say and how long we can take to say it.

Wiersbe: Charismatics have moved in that direction.

Bailey: Yes, they have.

Wiersbe: The charismatics have defrosted a lot of churches. We may not totally agree with their theology, but they have helped to bring new life to many churches.

Bailey: Especially in sermon delivery. They've helped to reignite the emotive aspect, which has been positive because it allows the whole person to worship and the whole person to preach. So I think that has enhanced preaching, because the participatory relationship between pulpit and pew enforces the creative moment. It results in adding creativity and spice to help get the people involved in the preaching experience. The freedom that the black preachers have always enjoyed I see spilling over into some of the white churches, especially, as you said, the charismatic churches.

The Place of Emotion and Emotionalism

Let's expand on that idea. What's the place of emotion in preaching, both positive and negative?

Wiersbe: Well, the negative of emotion is emotionalism, and we don't want that. We don't want ham actors in the pulpit. Emotionalism is artificial. It's made for the moment.

Bailey: Manipulative.

Wiersbe: It's when you stop communicating and start manipulating. That's so easy to do, even with an enthusiastic congregation. They'll go anyplace you lead them. The preacher needs the self-control that the Holy Spirit can give. There's always room for true emotion in worship and in preaching. To shed tears in the pulpit is not wicked, but in some churches, the people would be embarrassed.

Bailey: My people aren't ashamed of showing their emotions.

Wiersbe: My Swedish forebears were not afraid to cry publicly, but my German relatives were on the other end of the spectrum.

Bailey: Whether for good or ill, this is one of the lines of demarcation that has separated blacks and whites, because African-Americans historically have been and still are an emotional people. With us, celebration is a cultural thing, whether in church or at the football stadium. You can follow this all the way back to Africa. It wasn't until I visited Africa that I really began to understand why we are the way we are. For instance, wearing loud colors is an African tradition that we brought over with us. I don't necessarily agree with all these traditions, but you have to understand where they came from and what they mean. Even down to the bragging we do—"I'm the greatest!"

When Ricky Henderson won the base-stealing championship—he stole more bases than Lou Brock—and he lifted second base over his head, he was criticized for getting so emotional about it. There is a difference in the way blacks and white celebrate. White folks need to know that my people are emotional, not to show off or get attention but because that's the way we are. If what Phillips Brooks said in his Yale lecture is true, that preaching is truth proclaimed through personality, then we must make room for the pathos of the preacher just as much as we make room for the logos and ethos.

Soliciting Congregational Feedback

How do you obtain and encourage congregational feedback and responsiveness to the sermons?

Wiersbe: You read your mail, answer your phone, and don't stay at arm's length.

There's responsiveness both during the sermon and afterward. How do you encourage that kind of back and forth?

Wiersbe: I think that one of the keys is just plain openness to people. They realize you're not going to cut their throat if they say something negative. A. W. Tozer taught me a great lesson about criticism. He said, "Never be afraid of honest criticism. If the critic is right, he's helped you. If the critic is wrong, you can help him." Either way, somebody is helped. My best and most helpful feedback came from the staff and from the elders. They didn't feel that they had to pat me on the back or put me on a pedestal. They would talk quite frankly but lovingly. That was a big help to me. Our family can be a great help in this area.

Bailey: Sure. So far as the response to the preaching event, I think black preachers do have a unique experience, because we have the privilege to have a conversation within a conversation, while not losing sight of the first conversation as the second conversation is going on. Does that thoroughly confuse you?

Wiersbe: Well, the one conversation—pew to pulpit—enhances the other.

Bailey: One does enhance the other. While I'm preaching, I may stop and ask, "Have I got a witness? Are you still there? Do you hear what I'm saying?" But when I ask, "Do I have a witness?" I'm not really asking for a witness. I use it as a pacer. If I'm going too fast, it helps to slow me down. Or I use it as a pacer to give people time to intellectually breathe. Or I use it as a pacer to really ask for your support or to find out if you're paying attention. Black preachers have these two conversations going on at the same time. The conversation also builds a camaraderie that is just incredible between the pulpit and the pew. Now a lot of this has been dropped in some churches as our people have been exposed to the media and have heard other preachers, but by and large it still goes on. I still do it. But people are becoming more sensitive to the clock, so some of this two-way conversation may have to stop because of the time factor.

I don't get the kinds of letters that white pastors get. I've talked to some white pastors who tell me about the incredible letters they receive. When I initially began to receive a few letters, I was offended, because this was not a part of our history. I had some people from New York join our church. One lady had a Pentecostal background and wrote me, either with a compliment or a criticism, almost every Sunday. But some of her criticisms were on target, and I had to work my way through them because I wasn't accustomed to that sort of feedback. I finally called her in to sit down and talk about it, and she told me what her tradition was and I told her what mine was. She slowed her writing down to about once a month, but she kept it up. Once we had talked about it, I looked upon it much more favorably and accepted what she had to say. We eventually clashed over some doctrinal matters, and they left the church.

I don't think people have a right to criticize and remain anonymous; therefore, if a letter is signed, I'll read it and respond. If it is unsigned, my secretary reads it, and the letter usually ends up in the wastebasket. I've asked my secretary not to show me any anonymous mail.

Wiersbe: Dr. Harry Ironside, who pastored Moody Memorial Church in Chicago, used to say, "If it's not worth signing, it's not worth reading."

Bailey: Occasionally somebody will write and ask a real interesting question about the message, although we don't usually get a lot of feedback through the mail. What I've tried to do in the past to correct that was to pool together a preaching team that gives me evaluations and suggestions. Two of the members are my researchers; one of them is a member of my office staff, a lady, because I think it's important to get the female perspective.

Wiersbe: My wife sees things in the Bible that I don't see—and they're really there!

Bailey: A man and a woman can read the same text and never approach it the same way. So I'll ask her what she hears the text saying. And her input makes a lot of difference because most of our congregations have more women than men anyway. We constantly preach from the male side of the mental perspective, and it's important to hear what the women have to say.

As a congregation becomes more affluent, does that alter the back-and-forth conversation? Do parishioners become more sedate, more controlled?

Bailey: It can go either way. I know some African-American congregations that have become more sedate as they've become more affluent and better educated. It depends on how dear they hold their cultural background. The Concord Church is affluent and educated and adapts to all types of preaching, because the Word of God is central, yet we have not moved away from call and response. Despite the excess of some, and despite the massive rational, intellectual attack of the scholarly establishment, folk language has a way of clinging to the subtle wisdom and power that has been collected and funneled from generation to generation. So long as the generation's descendants speak the words, some portion of that original impact will insist on surviving. Per Dr. Henry Mitchell, the preacher who would tap this resource for redemptive contemporary ends needs only to join the life stream of the common folk and interpret the gospel from that population base's heritage, culture, and perspective. On the other hand, case in point, I know a black pastor friend who is as different from myself as night is from day, but our churches function in similar ways. The church I serve has more of an African-American culture, and where he serves has more of the flavor of the Eurocentric culture, but our churches offer a very similar approach to ministry. Both are committed to preaching the Word, but it's the "flavor" of the worship services and the philosophy of how to "do church" that makes us lean in two different cultural directions. People will make their decision based on what they're comfortable with.

Handouts and Testimonies

What about sermon handouts?

Wiersbe: Make them available the next week. If you put the outline in the bulletin, the sermon becomes predictable, the surprise element is lost, and you can't make any last-minute changes.

Bailey: When I give an outline, it's the kind where you fill in the blanks.

What about the use of testimonies in the service?

Bailey: We do it.

Does that help or enhance the preaching? What are some ways that you use testimonies?

Bailey: Whenever I'm doing stewardship preaching, I use testimonies that tie into the sermon. I mean, it's incredible what God leads some people to say and do. One young lady, in her early thirties, was telling us that she wanted to give, but when she looked at her budget with her financial planner it just was not there. She downsized. She moved to a smaller apartment and bought a smaller car so she could give to the Lord.

Wiersbe: Amen.

Bailey: And that just floored us in light of where this generation is, to make that kind of sacrifice to give. Well, one of my members told me I needed to hear this young lady's testimony. I called her and she told me her testimony. I said, "You're on next Sunday." The impact was absolutely incredible. I've also used testimonies in the middle of the sermon. You have to work with the people and tell them they have only two minutes. If you don't cut it off, we'll cut you off! I tell them to write out the testimony and don't add anything to it. I've had only one person go a little bit over, but most of the time they stick with it once I work with them.

Wiersbe: The power of personal testimony is a marvelous thing. A ninety-year-old member of our church gave witness to our college department—between five and six hundred students—about how the Lord taught him and his wife to give. He had five minutes to tell the story. He came hobbling out, sat down on a stool, and talked for five minutes. Do you know what the students did when he was through? They gave him a standing ovation! You'd have thought they were at a football game. When the witness is authentic, people will show respect.

Shortened Attention Spans

One of the shifts that affects preaching today is the short attention spans of the younger generations, especially those who watch MTV and who have hyperactive schedules. Should we shorten the length of sermons today? Is there a difference between the black and the white cultures when it comes to the length of services?

Wiersbe: Well, they need more time than we do.

Bailey: Again, we're talking about change, and I'm struggling with this very thing. But my struggle is leading me toward shortening the sermons, which is making my sermons tighter and more effective. This is also in line with the changing times, because the hour of yesterday is the thirty seconds of today.

Wiersbe: Nothing wrong with that.

Bailey: Well, no, there's not. These changes in society, and the expectations of the younger congregation that I'm preaching to, can work out positively for my own ministry. I'm struggling with that because I was born into a culture where our preachers have been free to do it their way, and maybe their way needed some adjusting. I think it is important that we take into consideration the times that we're preaching in and the people that we're preaching to, as well as the various generational needs we should address. I don't think that these factors should dictate everything we do, but I choose to address these factors because it's making my preaching more effective. That's the whole purpose of preaching.

Wiersbe: I wish every preacher could be on the radio for a year and learn how to say it right the first time. I used to tell my students not to be "airplane preachers" who circle and circle but never land. If we work at it, we can say it right the first time. I think the entire service needs to be more disciplined. At the church we attend, we added fifteen minutes to each of the three Sunday morning services, which meant people had to be there at eight o'clock for the first service. That extra fifteen-minute margin has made a wonderful difference, and nobody has complained about having to get there fifteen minutes earlier. The same people who have been late for thirty years are still late. Without dumbing down the liturgy or moving at the speed of light, we can tighten up the total service and allow more time for preaching. Another important thing is that we hit that pulpit running and not waste time on long introductions.

Embarrassing Moments

What's the most embarrassing thing that has happened to you when you were preaching?

Wiersbe: One of the embarrassing things that happened to me was caused by my own stupidity. I asked the congregation to turn to a reference that had no relationship whatsoever to the message. I had written down the wrong Scripture.

Bailey: The wrong Scripture. I've done that.

Wiersbe: My preaching professor, Dr. Charles Koller, used to tell us to get to church early each Sunday, make sure the participants in the service all have bulletins and know what's planned, and then check your references. Well, I didn't do that. I just said, "I'm sorry, folks, but this has nothing to do with my message." And we moved on.

Bailey: It's important to know how to recover from those kinds of mistakes and learn to laugh at yourself. If you're too serious about it, sometimes it will cause the whole sermon to bomb. When you laugh at yourself and call the people's attention to it, they'll laugh with you and not at you. In all my years of preaching without a manuscript, I have never had a memory lapse, but it happened to me one Sunday morning. I was preaching at the second service, and I could not recall the second point of my sermon. Fortunately, earlier in the week I had been watching Norman Vincent Peale on national television, and the same thing happened to him. He turned around and asked his assistant, "What is my second point?" And his assistant told him. In a similar fashion, when I forgot my second point, I turned around to my assistant, who always takes notes, and asked him what my second point was. My assistant immediately responded with the appropriate answer. I turned back to the congregation and said, "Ladies and gentlemen, my second point is . . . !" They fell out of their seats laughing, and we moved right on.

Wiersbe: But there's one little factor you've left out: you have stature as a preacher, and so does Dr. Peale. That helps. In fact, people may enjoy seeing an expert make a mistake!

Preaching for a Verdict

What about the idea of "preaching for a verdict"? Is that still valid today?

Wiersbe: Many churches no longer give invitations for the lost to come and trust Christ.

Bailey: Well, I still do it, and I think it is still very important.

Wiersbe: I agree with you.

Bailey: Some younger seminary graduates have been taught that the public invitation is no longer appropriate. People are told to fill out a card, or come back Monday night for personal help, or they're encouraged to write the pastor or see someone after the benediction. I have never felt comfortable moving away from a public appeal. I think it's biblical.

Wiersbe: That isn't to say that there aren't other approaches or that they don't work. But why deliver your soul for thirty minutes or more and then not give people an opportunity for a personal response?

Bailey: Remember the old adage: "When the hunter raises the gun, look for some game to fall." If God is moving in hearts because of the message, he can call them right then and there. Let's give folks an opportunity to respond to the call of Christ.

Wiersbe: The metaphor behind "preaching for a verdict" bothers me a bit. It's the picture of a lawyer confronting a jury that has the right to decide whether what we said was right or wrong. That's not the atmosphere that I want for preaching. Nobody has the right to vote on God's truth. To me, the metaphor of the invitation should be, "Come to the feast, come to the wedding! Don't stay where you are! Come to the feast!"

Bailey: In preaching we inform the mind and stir the heart, but we also need to bend the will. People don't change until the will has been bent. They must be willing to submit to God's Word and God's call. People do what they're moved and motivated to do, and that involves the mind, heart, and will. That's the key to the invitation.

Wiersbe: At Moody Church, we ended the service with a hymn, and it wasn't always one of the standard invitation hymns. I would invite anybody to come who sensed that God was calling. We had counselors ready to help them. After the service we held a visitors' reception, and we occasionally saw people come to Christ there. The elders would introduce visitors to me, and this gave me the opportunity to ask about their spiritual life. If at Pentecost, Peter had not called people to repent and believe but had offered to see them later that afternoon near the temple, I wonder if three thousand would have responded?

Bailey: At the same time, we should diversify the invitation, because there are people who can be reached through multiple approaches. Jesus told Peter to cast his net on the other side of the boat. If you fish with one pole, you're just going to catch one fish, however, if you use a net, you will have a better chance catching many fish at one time. Sometimes you need a net! Therefore, we use more than one approach to the invitation. We have people walking the aisles, we have response cards in the pews, and we also have what is called "Face to Face" at Concord, which is our reception for our guests.

Wiersbe: It also helps during the public invitation to have counselors up front to welcome those who come and to open the Word to them. Some of them should wait at the front after the service ends, just in case somebody is seeking help. Not all babies are born in public.

Bailey: If seekers prefer to fill out a card and leave it in the back of the pew, we follow up on that right away. At the guest reception the people have doughnuts and coffee, and not only do we tell them a little bit about who we are, but we also seek to explain who Christ is and the relationship he desires to have with them. Before they leave we offer another opportunity to accept Christ or make whatever commitment they need to make. Some people are more comfortable doing this in a smaller gathering. The younger people are very comfortable with filling out cards and leaving them in the back of the pew, but it is different in each generation.

Wiersbe: Regardless of how we call people to trust Christ, we need to remember that the harvest is the end of the age, not the end of the meeting. We'll meet people in heaven who came to Christ because of some ministry of ours, and we knew nothing about it. God's Word accomplishes God's work in God's time.

Changes through the Years

All of this seems to be a part of this matter of change. What are some of the big changes you've seen during your years of ministry?

Wiersbe: The ideal preacher fifty years ago expounded the Scriptures and gave you outlines and explanations. Today the emphasis in preaching is on meeting personal needs. When I was in seminary, the pastoral counseling movement was just taking hold. We read one book on the subject. But the impact of the pastoral counseling movement forced us to change our preaching and consider intent as well as content. I think that's the biggest change I've seen.

I think the second change is that local church ministry is no longer from the top down and only in the hands of the "experts," the trained preachers. A very healthy lay movement has developed and has greatly strengthened the church.

Bailey: The dominant changes in the African-American culture have been related to the struggle of having access to social and economic freedom. This struggle has been going on a long time, and as it has changed, our preaching has changed. We're now helping our people interpret the times in which we find ourselves, push back the horizons, and find out what the next steps should be. More African-American preachers have taken advantage of college and seminary training, and this has brought changes in the way we say things as we preach. Blacks have always preached salvation but didn't always use the same vocabulary as white evangelicals. I've met whites who didn't believe that blacks were saved, simply because we didn't use the traditional evangelical language. That's a horrible assumption to make. Even though we didn't express things the same way as the whites did, there was no question about the encounter our people have had with Jesus Christ. After going to school many of our preachers, including myself, have begun to use the best of the evangelical language. Some of the perceptions that were different in each of our cultures are now coming together because we're using the same language. The experience of salvation has always been there, but now we are starting to use the same language that communicates the salvific experience.

Wiersbe: It seems to me that the black church over these years has been countercultural in its opposition to the white establishment, whereas the white church has not been the light it should have been. Our white churches have been mirrors reflecting the values of the culture instead of lights exposing the sins of the culture.

Introducing Changes in Preaching

How do you introduce changes in preaching without losing your congregation? Are there ways to prepare your leaders and your members for changes in preaching?

Wiersbe: I've found that the best way to do something different in the pulpit is to introduce the change in another meeting. But don't keep doing it. Back off and then do it again. This enables you to test the waters. But if you're talking about major changes, then you'll have to sit down with your leaders and explain both the theology and the philosophy of the changes. If there's a book available that deals with these changes, have the leaders read it and then discuss it on a retreat. We must take a nonaggressive, nonmilitant posture so they don't think we're declaring war on some cherished tradition.

Bailey: I think that method is very good for making changes within the church's structure and program. However, in the African-American church the pulpit is the driving force for change. If seeds are not planted in the Word of God from the pulpit, they will seldom take root in the heart of the congregation.

Wiersbe: I'd have to say to my leaders, "Brethren, from time to time you're going to hear me approaching some texts from what you would call a social-action angle. We all believe it's biblical to preach about the sins of society. I'm not preaching some social gospel, but I am trying to apply the gospel to social needs." I'd want to be wise as a serpent but harmless as a dove.

Bailey: I do think that we should do some grunt work in this book for those pastors who have a heart but don't have a clue. How do I develop the same core values in my leadership? I tease the young preachers at our church with a quote: "First Bailey chapter one, verse one, 'There is a way that seemeth right to the young pastor, but the end thereof is to get put out.'"

Wiersbe: There's a difference between cosmetic changes—a new bulletin cover—and structural changes such as a whole new liturgy or a new organizational plan. Wise is that pastor who knows the difference and is unwilling to sacrifice his ministry just to achieve a small victory. We must have the right perspective and the right timing, or we'll create more problems than we'll solve. Also, when you make changes, you have to study the ripple effect. Who are the people affected? How will they respond? Will the changes be misunderstood?

Picture a church that's been very traditional. The minister always sat on the platform, they followed the same order of service week after week, and he preached the same way every Sunday. Now this young pastor comes to the church and wants to introduce a testimony in the middle of his sermon. Or maybe he wants to back up the sermon with drama or do some first-person narrative preaching. What's your counsel?

Wiersbe: Whether he's young or old, the new pastor should take time to get to know the people of the church, and especially the leadership, and to find out how changes are made in the church. Who are the people with the authority—and they aren't always the officers! If changes are forced from the outside, people will react negatively; but if they grow from the inside, they have a better chance of being accepted. The pastor who makes all those changes at once is in for trouble.

Bailey: I agree. The only thing that will change will be his address.

Wiersbe: Change for the sake of change is nothing but novelty. Change for the sake of better ministry and greater outreach is progress. You can build a crowd with novelty, but you can't build a church.

Bailey: In the African-American church the preacher has greater influence and authority, and the leadership generally supports that kind of pulpit freedom if the pastor decided to change his approach. One exception might be if he moved the pulpit. That might create a problem, but even that is not the cardinal sin. But if preaching changes started to bleed over from the pulpit into the various programs and auxiliaries of the church—where things are very traditional and institutionalized—and the pastor tries to make sweeping changes there, then he would run into conflict.

Wiersbe: Church groups and officers can be very territorial. It's human nature. I heard about a Sunday school class that sued the church for asking them to move out of their room to another room. The class had bought and laid the carpeting, they had decorated the room and purchased furniture, and they had no plans to relocate.

Bailey: I know a church that had a battle with the Sunday school because the people were paying their tithes to their Sunday school classes and not to the church during the regular offertory period. Each adult class had a bank account separate from that of the church. The church mortgage was about to be foreclosed, and the Sunday school told the church, "That's your problem."

Wiersbe: Organizational problems are basically spiritual problems. Like some family problems, they're solved as the children grow up and get a mature outlook on things. The pastor needs to be patient and prayerful. We don't like to say it, but sometimes a funeral or somebody leaving the church helps to solve a problem.

CHAPTER 7

PUTTING IT
INTO PRACTICE

A   *s we approached the end of our time together, we wanted to consider how the insights we had shared might be implemented in churches across the land. So we asked E. K., How can preachers become more ethnically sensitive? Can you think of any examples or personal experiences that illustrate how we can become more sensitive and concerned and develop an increased appreciation for diversity? Listen to the unexpected and revealing answer that follows.*

A Shotgun in the Stomach

Bailey: There is a history behind every attitude. Allow me to share with you an almost life-shattering experience that left me with a very negative attitude. While traveling to Los Angeles, California, in the summer of 1963 with four of my high school football buddies, I received one of those Rodney King–type beatings at the hands of two white police officers. This all came about as a result of me trying to flag down the policemen to ask for directions. It spiraled out of control from there. After surprisingly breaking out of the officer's deadly choke hold on me, his partner immediately aimed his double-barreled shotgun at my stomach. They later claimed they misunderstood my hand waving as taunting them. I am truly blessed to be alive today.

I shared this experience in order to verbally demonstrate the power of preaching the Bible. As you may well imagine, that experience left me with a very negative attitude toward white people. All of us possess the tendency to project upon a whole race the faults of a few people, and that is exactly what I did. Although I grew up in the southern segregated city of San Antonio, Texas, the tragic experience in California was by far the most devastating of my young life. After that experience I proceeded through many years embracing both the positive and negative aspects of the black power movement. Recently, in the 1990s, we went through another social wave called Afrocentrism, and again I was greatly influenced by the movement.

During the mid-1990s, as I was in the process of preaching through the book of Ephesians, God revealed to me my reactionary racism. He also revealed to me that I must follow his pattern for biblical reconciliation in order to fully represent him. Prior to that point, I was able to dialogue with white people without showing my inner anger. However, I was still not ready to do what it took to bring about racial reconciliation. Through the preaching process, God deeply convicted me, so much that I took the initiative to both seek personal reconciliation and lead the church I am pastoring to seek racial reconciliation.

Two or three years before moving to our present location, the Lord led me to preach and teach our congregation what it means to be a part of the true body of Christ. We are reconciled to God by the death of his Son on the cross and by his blood—that is the message of these Scriptures. According to Ephesians 2:16: "and might reconcile both groups to God in one body, through the cross." Since Jesus has received us, he commands that we must receive one another, regardless of race, color, creed, or gender.

Opposition to this new direction was minimal, and that quickly subsided as we lifted high the authority of the Word of God. As pastor my position was, Will we be a biblical church, or will we be a social club? There was a choice to be made. Either we could govern the church by our personal biases and negative experiences or we could govern the church by the biblical authority of the Word of God.

At the time of this theological reengineering and social realignment, we had only one consistent white member and her family. I am sure they felt very uncomfortable many Sundays as I spewed my racial venom from the pulpit. God only knows how they remained as members through it all. As a result of my personal transformation, my wife and I have become very dear friends to this member and her African-American husband. In fact, we share in a monthly home forum, where her husband is the facilitator. The home forum includes not only African-American members from the Concord Church but also white members from several of our leading white churches in the city, such as Prestonwood Baptist and Park Cities Baptist Church. Together we have been able to have an impact on critical issues within the city. For that I am grateful.

I am sure that many African-Americans share similar testimonies as mine. I do not know many African-American males who have not had some kind of negative conflict with some law enforcement agent. Few African-American men have not been victims of racial profiling, where they have been stopped, questioned, or searched for no other apparent reason than the color of their skin. Some unfortunately have experienced far greater harassment and confrontation beyond that of racial profiling. Therefore, it takes the literal power of the Holy Spirit not only to convert the heart in a relationship with Christ but also to transform the heart in the matter of racial reconciliation.

Can we develop ethnic sensitivity by cultivating a friendship across the culture?

Wiersbe: But fraternizing with "the enemy" never stays hidden, does it?

Black Pastor in a Lily-White Church

Bailey: Yes, I do believe that it is possible to cultivate ethnic sensitivity by developing quality friendships across cultural and racial lines. Immediately two people come to mind when I consider friendships across racial lines. First, there is Jim Denison. He is the pastor of the Park Cities Baptist Church in Dallas. Upon arriving to pastor Park Cities, Jim told me he asked his deacons to recommend the name of an African-American pastor with whom he might forge a friendship. They gave him my name. So Jim called and invited me to lunch, and upon meeting we hit it off. He took the initiative to extend his hand in friendship. I was a bit cautious, not knowing him, and it took a little while, but we became fast friends. We decided to meet monthly for either breakfast or lunch, which we have continued to do. Jim invited my wife and me to conduct a marital enrichment seminar for his church. It was a wonderful experience. He also extended to me the privilege of preaching the two morning services that same weekend. We still have breakfast once a month.

Jim and his wife have visited in our home, especially during my illness, to encourage us. We talk about books that we have read. He has also been a guest at our International Conference on Expository Preaching. He preached a marvelous sermon there last year and literally swept the brothers off their feet. They were very encouraged to be blessed by the marvelous preaching and by an even greater individual.

Jim's wife, Jana, and my wife, Sheila, have become faster friends. Together they served on a board that brought Anne Graham Lott to the city. They pray together, and they have developed a very strong friendship, even separate from that of Jim and myself. It has been a great model for anyone seeking to develop a friendship across racial lines.

It has taken more than breakfast once a month. It has required risk and consistency, but the risks have been worth the rewards. Whatever I'm doing out here, he will support it if he has the time, and I'll do the same for him.

Wiersbe: To do that, we need an attitude of faith and love and a lot of confidence in the Lord. I can think of some pastors whose first response to an invitation might be, "What's your game?"

Bailey: Well, I'm not above that either.

Wiersbe: Nor am I. White preachers do it too.

Bailey: But we have to plow on through all that. Let me make it clear: it was not E. K. Bailey's choice. The Spirit of God convicted me of this, and I know the Spirit of God can do that in anyone. Maybe God knew I was at the point of readiness. I think that might have something to do with it. And I know that the years of expounding the Word laid a foundation for it. So because of what he's done in my life in the past, God knew that here is a person who will lead and do what I ask him to do, and it will impact others.

I confess that I've been skeptical of whites who came to me, reaching out, because we all have been bitten and deceived, and we have asked, "Okay, what's your game? What are you pushing?" But consistency makes the difference, along with transparency.

Another friend whom I consider to be genuine is Mike Fechner, the founder and president of H.I.S. Bridge Builders Ministries in Dallas. He is also the adult pastor on staff at the Prestonwood Baptist Church in Plano, Texas. Mike and I became acquainted through a mutual friend. He introduced us, and we hit it off as we did ministry work together in Turner Court in South Dallas. Unfortunately, both of us were disappointed to discover some unethical conduct on the part of our mutual friend, so subsequently we had to disassociate ourselves from him.

Ironically, Mike and I remained friends. Immediately I noticed that Mike was genuine. In the African-American community, to call someone of another race "genuine" is to say a mouthful. First, it says that he does not come with the typical white agenda that we see being practiced so often in the African-American community. Second, Mike did not come with a prescribed idea about what we needed in our community. Third, he did not come with the attitude that here is a white man who has the solution to all of the problems in the African-American community. In terms of his attitude, he simply came as a humble brother who genuinely loved God and people. He prayed for God to guide him to the right people that he could partner with, who also had the same goals and desires to help this disenfranchised and disinherited African-American community.

I could tell Mike was genuine when he walked into the homes of the people in the projects and sat down and ate their food. I knew he was genuine when he hugged little snotty-nosed black children. He cared for them as though they were his own. I knew he was genuine when he took his own family to fellowship, socialize, and have fun with children who were undereducated and exposed to drugs and every unimaginable thing you could experience in society. I knew he was genuine when he asked the men of our church and the men of his church, at that time in far North Dallas, to come way down to the projects in lower South Dallas to meet and have fellowship over breakfast. But more importantly, they came to strategize about how to evangelize the area as well as provide resources to meet the physical needs of the people in these projects.

Soon Mike moved from calling me his friend to calling me his brother, and doing so in public. It made me feel a little uncomfortable at first, because people would chuckle. But Mike rolled right on as though he had no idea what they were laughing about. I was slower in calling Mike my brother. My attitude was that you are a nice fellow and seem worthy of friendship, but as a white man, you will have to prove yourself before you can move into the fraternity of being called brother. There are many black men that I do not call brother, yet here is a white man calling me brother. So it was just a little uneasy calling him brother. But he did just that and was honest and forthright in every aspect of our relationship.

When I needed him when I was sick, he was there. He came and prayed for me and led others throughout the city in prayer for me. Everyone knew that if you wanted to know how I was doing, all you had to do was ask Mike, because he checked on me regularly. When Mike went through an especially devastating crisis, I was there to pray with him and help provide guidance as he made some critical decisions. Our friendship grew to the point where he asked me to serve on the board of his organization, H.I.S. Bridge Builders Ministries, and I also asked him to serve on the board of my organization, E. K. Bailey Ministries, Inc. We help counsel each other and raise funds for each other's organizations.

I have invited Mike to come and preach at our church and to serve in several capacities in our worship experience. We have given our testimony together at reconciliation meetings in the city. He invited me to speak at his Sunday school class, one of the largest at Prestonwood Baptist Church in Dallas. He was also instrumental in getting me invited to speak to three thousand singles at Metro on a Monday night. Metro is a citywide nondenominational Bible study offered to university students and young professionals. Metro's goal is to provide an atmosphere that produces community, worship, and growth. Because of Mike's extraordinary prayer life and incredible faith, he is the most positive person I know. His positive attitude just overflows onto anyone who comes into his presence. He directs everyone to look to the Lord and pray about his or her circumstances and watch God work it out. I tell Mike all the time to not allow seminary training to mess up his beautiful and godly faith.

One of the ways that our friendship has made us more sensitive toward each other is that we have discussed it. Our friendship has reached the point where we can discuss our racial and ethnic differences. Several times I have said to Mike, "That's a no-no in the African-American community. You don't refer to African-Americans that way, or you don't say that to one of our people." Out of sheer ignorance, he would make certain insensitive statements, but I knew his heart and that what was coming out of his mouth was simply what he had been trained or exposed to. I would gently share with him a more acceptable way to communicate his idea, and he would do the same for me when some of my latest racism would ooze out. Not only did we become more sensitive to our own racial differences but also to the idiosyncrasies of each other's race and culture.

Both Mike and I, along with our wives, participate in a home forum where we discuss racial issues and primarily how the power of the Holy Spirit and the Word of God can lead us to overcome our racial biases and prejudices. In this home forum we watch movies and do research on historical and contemporary issues impacting our society. We also read books together and go to meetings together that deal with reconciliation. It is a blessed experience.

Another aspect I consider to be a part of a quality friendship is the ability to remain friends through disagreement. We differed strongly on some political issues and on issues that he was involved with in his church. Now, that was the test that will either make or break it. Again he took the initiative as he said, "E. K., you're my brother, and I'm not going to allow this to separate me from you." We can't say, "You can be my friend until we disagree over critical issues. Then we separate along racial or political lines." It did not happen. We fought our way through and remained committed to each other. We didn't allow the disagreement to destroy our friendship. In the past, particularly with white Christian friends, if there was a disagreement over a theological or social issue, the friendship went down the drain. However, I can honestly say that while Mike and I have had those kinds of disagreements, praise God, our friendship remains steadfast.

Wiersbe: Do you still disagree?

Bailey: Oh, yes! We still disagree, but we got over the emotional chasm that was starting to separate us.

We talked about examples in personal life, but is there a way to use the pulpit to encourage this kind of cross-cultural reconciliation and cooperation?

Wiersbe: One of the themes of Ephesians is that God is putting things together in Jesus Christ (Eph. 1:10). He's reconciling sinners to himself, and Jews and Gentiles, and people in the church. If we preach all the counsel of God faithfully, we have to deal with our own personal reconciliation with others.

I attended an integrated high school. The blacks and whites were in athletic events together, and I had two black friends as locker partners. My first taste of segregation was when our debate team went to downstate Indiana. One of our best debaters was an African-American fellow, a brilliant guy, and they wouldn't let him into the restaurant. This was in the forties in southern Indiana.

When I went to Kentucky to pastor, in a city hall building in western Kentucky I saw segregated restrooms for the first time. Then I went to Moody Church, which was like preaching to the United Nations. I really didn't have to change my attitudes, because I wasn't a segregationist, but it was the beginning of a new challenge as we worked together. But I think the greatest push I got was at the E. K. Bailey preaching conference. They accepted me and even listened to me preach.

How E. K. and Warren Met

How did you two happen to meet?

Bailey: It was at the Beeson Divinity School's pastors' conference in Birmingham. Dr. Manuel Scott was scheduled to speak but got sick and recommended me as his replacement. When I got there and realized that Warren Wiersbe was the other preacher, I tried to find an excuse to leave town. But he was courteous and said some encouraging words, and we immediately became friends. So during the week, when I got enough nerve, I said, "I have a preaching conference, and we're trying to expose African-American preachers to the skill of doing expository preaching. Will you come?" He said, "Of course." That started it, and our friendship has continued to grow.

Wiersbe: I confess that I brought to the Beeson conference some prejudices about black preachers, but E. K.'s preaching that week destroyed them all. He had both heat and light, content and intent. It did my soul good. The expository preaching conference has been an annual spiritual transfusion for me.

Bailey: Back to my bridge building with local white pastors. Sharing your own experiences might be a good first step in getting your church involved. It's also a good way to get other pastors doing the same thing. But I keep my leaders informed about my pastoral friendships and also about the home forum where I meet with white families. When people ask what's happening, I say, "Well, it's coming, it's coming. We're working on it." So even without my talking a lot about it, the people are seeing the friendships that are being developed and know they will lead to something good.

You're modeling reconciliation for them as well as preaching reconciliation to them.

Bailey: Preaching reconciliation challenges us that it should happen, and modeling reconciliation assures us that it can happen.

The Place of Prayer

Wiersbe: One area that we often forget is our public prayers. Years ago I encouraged our pastor to pray each Sunday for another church in town, and the practice goes on. I wonder how many white churches prayed publicly for the King family and the movement he led when Martin Luther King was killed.

Bailey: Or how many white churches prayed for President Clinton when he was going through his crisis? And how many black churches are going to pray for President Bush?

Wiersbe: But it has to happen.

Bailey: That's true. Maybe if you and I keep it up, others will follow.

Where do we go from here? Richard Farmer suggests that we stand at the perilous edge between our past and the future. "Our greatest peril may be our failure to appreciate the wondrous contributions of the people of color to the fabric of the universal body of Christ." He concludes by saying, "We see all our talk about unity die as empty words and our high ideals destroyed by our narrowness. I still believe that this period will pass. I reach confidently into the future."[5]

Having completed our time of talking together, it's now time to act. How do the ideas discussed flesh out when applied to a sermon? What if both Warren Wiersbe and E. K. Bailey preached on the same text of Scripture? That's what happens in the next section of the book. Turn the page and see how a black preacher and a white preacher handle the same text.

---

[5]Farmer, "African-American Worship," p. 131.

PART 2

WE PREACH TOGETHER

CHAPTER 8

TESTIMONY OF
A TAX COLLECTOR

Luke 19:1–10

E. K. Bailey

Then Jesus entered and passed through Jericho. Now behold, there was a man named Zacchaeus who was a chief tax collector, and he was rich. And he sought to see who Jesus was, but could not because of the crowd, for he was of short stature. So he ran ahead and climbed up into a sycamore tree to see Him, for He was going to pass that way. And when Jesus came to the place, He looked up and saw him, and said to him, 'Zacchaeus, make haste and come down, for today I must stay at your house.' So he made haste and came down, and received Him joyfully. But when they saw it, they all complained, saying, 'He has gone to be a guest with a man who is a sinner.'

"Then Zacchaeus stood and said to the Lord, 'Look, Lord, I give half of my goods to the poor; and if I have taken anything from anyone by false accusation, I restore fourfold.'

"And Jesus said to him, 'Today salvation has come to this house, because he also is a son of Abraham; for the Son of Man has come to seek and to save that which was lost'" (Luke 19:1–10, NKJV).

The transcript of this sermon has been edited and is shorter than the original delivered sermon.

One of the benefits that we experience growing up in a local church is the various and vivacious assortment of songs, rhymes, games, and couplets which indelibly stamp the names of biblical characters upon the fabric of our memories. As we delve in the corridors of our mind, many of us will remember this rhyme:

> Zacchaeus was a wee little man,
> And a wee little man was he.
> He climbed up in a sycamore tree,
> For the Lord he wanted to see.
> But as the Savior passed that way,
> He looked up in the tree,
> And he said,
> "Zacchaeus, you come down,
> For I'm going to your house today."

I've always wondered what drove Zacchaeus to climb that tree; what was his motivation, what compelled him to climb that tree? For it is exceedingly unusual, imaginatively unlikely, and totally uncanny to see a well-dressed, well-educated, well-established, wealthy man at midday, publicly but shamelessly climbing a tree, crawling out on its branches, and hanging on a limb. What led him to ignore embarrassment, disregard shame, reject ridicule, and do something as uncharacteristic as climbing a tree for all to see?

In order to answer this and many other questions, I invite you to take a journey with me. We must travel to the backside of the Roman Empire, penetrate the sweltering, fly-infested land of Palestine, traverse the difficult terrain of the Holy Land, and then enter the fragrance-filled city of Jericho, where we will find the home of this despicable and despised tax collector named Zacchaeus.

We need to rise early in the morning and travel with this man to observe the things he has encountered as he attempted to collect taxes. As he traveled, he pulled out his Day-Timer to check the names and addresses of the people he planned to see that day.

It wasn't long before he arrived at his first scheduled appointment. He noticed that it was an unkempt dilapidated shanty, desperately in need of some paint and major repairs. There was no sympathy or mercy coming from Zacchaeus. The only thing that was of any importance was the word *overdue* stamped by the person's name. He knocked on the door. As the door swung open, it croaked and groaned with the eeriness of an Alfred Hitchcock movie. On the other side stood a frail blind man.

The blind man asked, "Who's there?" And Zacchaeus answered, "I'm here to collect the taxes you owe the Roman government." In a trembling voice, the blind man began to explain his inability to pay his taxes. He said, "I have no family. I don't receive any pension. And there's no society to help the blind. I want to pay you, but right now I am not able to pay. But please, I beg you, have mercy, Mr. Zacchaeus. Give me thirty days. I don't know how or where, but somehow I'll find the money."

Zacchaeus was caught between money and mercy. Zacchaeus said to the blind man, "That's not usually my style, but you have thirty days. But blind man, when I get back, if you don't show me the money, you'll not only be blind, but you'll be homeless." Zacchaeus turned, and as he walked away, he thought to himself, "That didn't go very well; perhaps I'll have better luck at the next house."

He came to his next appointment, and he pounded ferociously on the door. As the woman slowly opened the door, Zacchaeus grimaced as he recognized that there was going to be a problem. The woman's complexion was completely discolored; it was whitish-yellow, as if all the blood had been drained from her face. Her eyes seemed as if they were being sucked out of their sockets, her lips were cracked and swollen, her cheekbones were disfigured and repulsively protruded from her face, and her hair was dry, trashy, and matted. Her face was wet with tears. Her speech was slurred as she said, "I know who you are and why you've come. But Mr. Zacchaeus, O Mr. Zacchaeus, I don't have any way of paying my taxes. You see, for twelve years I've had a blood disorder. In that time my insurance was canceled, my husband divorced me, and my savings account is empty. I have pawned my jewelry and furniture, and everything in my checking account is spent. But give me thirty days, just thirty days; all I need is at least thirty days."

Zacchaeus was now caught between greed and grace. He said, "For some reason I feel benevolent today. You have thirty days. But when I return, I want the taxes." And as he walked away, he thought to himself, "Maybe I'll have better luck at the next house."

As Zacchaeus walked around the bend, there stood the third house. A woman stood catatonic and listless in front of the house. She stared into space, not seeming to recognize that he was moving closer to her. When he tried to speak to her, there was no response. Suddenly there was a blood-curdling scream that sent shivers up his spine. Zacchaeus whirled to see where the scream came from. On the hillside across the street, running nude between the stones in the graveyard, cutting himself, was the silhouette of what looked like a cross between a man and a wild animal.

Suddenly the woman broke her silence. "That used to be my husband," she said. "He was a good man. I'm still praying that one day he'll be restored and return to his family. Some have suggested that I should move on with my life, but I still love him. He's the father of my children. I'm not sure if it will ever happen, because no man can tame him and no man can bind him. He calls himself Legion because he's possessed by many demons." Now Zacchaeus was caught between dollars and demons.

Not anxious to dialogue with demons, Zacchaeus began to reverse. Before the woman said anything about the taxes, Zacchaeus said, "I'll be back in your area in thirty days. Be prepared to pay upon my return."

He hurriedly turned away as his heart was still palpitating. He looked in his Day-Timer, and there was one last house to visit. When he arrived, there was a funeral spray hanging on the door, suggesting that someone had died. But not even a family tragedy would stop Zacchaeus, so he knocked anyway. A grieving woman, veiled and dressed in black, answered the door. She said, "I know who you are and why you've come. Zacchaeus, my son died yesterday, and I'm on my way to the funeral. I had to use the tax money to bury my only son." Zacchaeus said, "I've already given some of your neighbors thirty days. So I'll be back in thirty days." Again Zacchaeus was trapped between the law and love.

The thirty days passed quickly. Zacchaeus left home at the crack of dawn, as he did every day. He opened his Day-Timer and noticed that this was the day he was to return to those four homes—those houses that represented the most unproductive day in his career as a tax collector. He squared his shoulders, and as he walked, you could hear him say, "No sob story will dissuade me today. They will either pay, surrender their property, or be thrown in prison."

At the first house he noticed a significant change. The grass had been manicured. The house had undergone extensive renovation. He knocked on the door. Zacchaeus was mesmerized when a man opened the door. He had a piercing gaze and a voice that boomed with astounding authority. Zacchaeus said, "I'm sorry, sir, but I'm looking for the man of the house, the blind man." The man said, "I am the man of the house." Zacchaeus answered, "No, I was here thirty days ago, and the man I spoke with was blind." The man said, "I'm that man. I was blind. Mr. Zacchaeus, let me explain to you my story. One day a man told me that Jesus was coming to town, and I ran uptown. I knew it might be my only chance to meet him. When Jesus was passing by I heard all the commotion. I asked, 'What's happening?' They said, 'Jesus is passing by.' And I yelled, 'Jesus, son of David, have mercy on me!' The townspeople, the mayor, and the council said, 'Hush, you're making a nuisance of yourself. You're embarrassing the town.' But I cried even louder, 'Jesus! Son of David, have mercy on me!' They tried to push me into the background, but I knew this was my only chance. I cried louder still, 'Jesus! Son of David, have mercy on me!'"

The man said, "Zacchaeus, do you have time? Sit down and let me tell you what happened, for I have a testimony to tell. This is the way it was:

> "Amazing grace, how sweet the sound
> That saved a wretch like me.
> I once was lost, but now I'm found.
> I was blind, but now I see."

As Zacchaeus walked away, he thought, "This is some day! A man who was blind but now can see." Zacchaeus mused to himself, "One day I hope I will meet Jesus. Maybe Jesus can do something about my condition. That man said that this world's God has blinded the minds of unbelievers so they cannot see the light of the gospel or the glory of Christ, who is the image of God." Zacchaeus muttered aloud, "I hope I can see Jesus someday."

Upon arriving at the second house, Zacchaeus knocked on the door, and this beautiful woman, radiant with joy, answered. She had color in her cheeks, a glitzy glimmer in her eyes. She had a new hairdo. Her nails had been freshly manicured. Yes, she was styling. "Mr. Zacchaeus, it's good to see you," she purred, smiling effortlessly and glamorously. Zacchaeus said, "I'm looking for the woman of the house." She said, "I am the woman of the house." "Wait a minute. Do you know your blind neighbor down the street?" "Yes, I know him. But he's not blind anymore." Zacchaeus said, "I know. He paid his taxes today." She answered, "He didn't tell you? He sold his seeing-eye dog."

The woman said, "Zacchaeus, when I told you to come back in thirty days, that was nothing but a ploy. I was confident that in thirty days I would be dead. In fact, I had been praying to die. I thought that only death could deliver me from that unbearable existence. But a friend told me that Jesus was coming to town.

"I elbowed my way through the suffocating crowd. When I got close enough, I stretched out and was just able to touch the hem of his garment. And the moment I touched him, the blood that had been flowing for twelve years immediately dried up! But not only was my body healed; my soul was made whole. Even though my faith was inadequate, he made it sufficient." Zacchaeus said, "I don't know how much of this I can take—a blind man who can see, a dying woman who's full of life . . ." She said, "Zacchaeus, I know it's hard to believe, but I need to tell you what happened.

> *"I've had some good days. I've had some hills to climb.*
> *I've had some weary days and some sleepless nights.*
> *But when I look around and think things over,*
> *All of my good days outweigh my bad days. I won't complain.*
> *The Lord has been good to me, He's been so good to me,*
> *More than this old world could ever be. He's been good to me!*

"Zacchaeus, no more doctor bills and no more prescriptions to fill. I've been able to save a little money. Like my old ex-blind friend, here's the money for your taxes."

Zacchaeus turned sharply and headed toward the third house. He thought, "This is a weird and wacky day. I wonder if I will ever meet Jesus. Like that woman, I've had some long-standing, ever-present problems. I've had some painful experiences. Maybe if I met Jesus, he would do something about my problems."

Soon he was in front of that third house. He looked for the woman to be standing at the front of the house. But she was not there. When he knocked on the door, the woman answered. But before they could start talking, this handsome, young man walked out from behind her. Zacchaeus' first thought was, "I'm glad this woman got a new man. She should have kicked that old grave dweller to the curb."

About the same time, the woman spoke up: "Mr. Zacchaeus, I want you to meet my husband. You haven't met this man, because when you were here thirty days ago, his home was in the graveyard. But look at him now. Doesn't he look good? He's clothed and in his right mind. Mr. Zacchaeus, I owe you an apology. Thirty days ago I told you that no man could tame him and that no man could bind him, but that was before Jesus stepped off the boat. When Jesus walked in, the demons walked out. Look at him. He's a new man.

"Mr. Zacchaeus, if you want to be a new man, you must meet Jesus. He'll give you a new relationship with God, with yourself, and with your family. Old things will pass away, and behold, all things will become new. My husband met Jesus, and his life has been forever changed."

The man broke in and said, "Wait a minute. She can tell you some parts of the story, but it is my testimony. She didn't experience it like I experienced it; therefore let me tell you. Sit down, Zacchaeus. You can't stand up and listen to this. I need to tell you what happened.

> "I know I've been changed.
> I know I've been changed.
> I know I've been changed.
> The Angels in the Heavens done signed my name.
> I know I've been changed."

As Zacchaeus left, he thought to himself, "A blind man who can now see, a dying helpless woman who's now healed and full of life, and a demon-possessed man who has been delivered. Now I wonder if someday I will ever meet Jesus. I've got some demons hounding my heels. Maybe if I meet Jesus, I too will be delivered."

At the last house he thought rather sarcastically, "I wonder what surprise they will have for me." When he knocked on the door, the cutest little boy with the widest smile opened the door.

Zacchaeus said, "I'm sorry. I'm at the wrong house. There is no little boy that lives in the house that I'm looking for. Ironically, thirty days ago the woman of the house was on her way to bury her only son." The boy said, "Are you Mr. Zacchaeus? My mother has been expecting you. She said that you'd be back in thirty days. And Mom had said you're never late collecting the taxes."

Zacchaeus was startled. His heartbeat increased dramatically, and blood rushed to his head. He paused and gazed steadily at the boy, and then he tersely said, "Wait a minute. This could never be the house where that little boy died."

The boy said, "Mr. Zacchaeus, I'm that boy. I died. My mama's worst fear was that the disease that took my daddy and my older brother would someday take me. And thirty days ago my mama's worst fear came true. I got real sick. And my mother prayed for me.

She stayed by my bedside all day and all night. But God chose not to heal me, and I died. My mother had saved the money to pay you, but she had to use that money on my funeral. As the mourners led the procession out of Nain, there was another procession going in. And the procession of death collided with the procession of deity. Now, Mr. Zac, you know that death and deity cannot occupy the same space. You know that Jesus never attended a funeral. He never preached at a funeral. Every time he showed up, he transformed the funeral into a resurrection. And there we were at the gate—death versus deity. You should have seen the fireworks when death collided with deity. Jesus laid his resurrecting hand on me, and suddenly something began to stir in my lifeless body. I came back to life, Mr. Zac! When I sat up in the casket, it scared the undertaker so bad that he pushed me on out of the casket, took his casket back, and gave my mother her money back. Mr. Zac, here's the money for your taxes."

By the time the little boy finished talking, his mother came out. She said, "He's only twelve. He doesn't know much about life's deeper realities, so let me tell you like only a mother can tell you. Sit down. Do you have a little time, Mr. Zacchaeus? Let me tell you what happened." He said, "Tell me what happened." She said,

> *"Great is thy faithfulness, O God, my Father.*
> *There is no shadow of turnings in thee.*
> *Thou changest not, thy compassions they fail not.*
> *As thou has been, thou forever will be.*
> *Great is thy faithfulness. Great is thy faithfulness.*
> *Morning by morning new mercies I see.*
> *All I have needed, thy hand hath provided.*
> *Great is thy faithfulness, Lord, unto me."*

As Zacchaeus left, he thought, "A blind man who can see, a dying woman who's full of life, a demon-possessed man who has been delivered, and a dead boy that's been resurrected."

Zacchaeus closed his Day-Timer. On his way home he passed a friend who said, "Hey, Zac, have you heard?" Zacchaeus answered, "I've heard all I can handle for one day."

His friend said, "Jesus is in town!"

Zacchaeus said, "He is! I need to see him; I must see him!"

The man said, "You'd better hurry. He'll be leaving soon."

And as Zacchaeus' little feet pitter-pattered along the dusty road, he pondered about all his life experiences. And he mumbled to himself, "I wonder if this is my chance to meet Jesus. All of my life I've been a successful failure. I've been a paradox of prosperity and poverty. I'm rich in the things of this world, but poor in the things of God. I've had a tough and terrible life, even though to many people everything seems gloriously well. At a glance I look like the fulfillment of every man's dream. But what they don't know is that sometimes when you get to the top of the ladder, you discover that it's leaning against the wrong building. Maybe Jesus can do something about the emptiness that fills my soul.

"I have another problem. I've been a short man in a tall world, and I have always thought that it was the shortness of my stature that created all of my problems. But maybe if I meet Jesus, he will help me to understand who I really am. Because I'm beginning to see as I search my heart that it's not the shortness of my stature but the shortness of my relationship with God that has caused my heart to be cold, callous, and uncompassionate. Maybe if I meet Jesus, he will change my heart and my life."

So Zacchaeus ran toward town. When he got there he couldn't see over the dense crowd. So finally he decided to run ahead of Jesus and the crowd. As he ran, that's when he saw that tree. Remember, I had wondered what led him to climb that tree. It became clear that the reason was not the shortness of his stature, but it was a seething soul that could only find sufficiency and satisfaction in the Savior. Also, Zacchaeus climbed that tree because he remembered what Jesus had done in the lives of other people, and he was utterly aware of the urgent changes that needed to occur in his own life.

As though this were a scene from *Spider Man,* in a single leap Zacchaeus swung up into the tree. It was at that moment that Jesus came by and saw him, and he said, "Zacchaeus, you come down, for I'm going to your house today." Isn't it good to know that Jesus knows what tree you are up and what limb you are on? And he will call you down! Zacchaeus slid down his tree of despair, Zacchaeus slid down his tree of pride, and Zacchaeus slid down his tree of guilt and decided that for the rest of his life he would walk with Jesus under the tree of salvation.

Zacchaeus' first thought at the foot of the tree was, "I've got to invite him home with me, because Jesus always makes a difference when he goes home with you. In fact, if he doesn't go home with you, he doesn't go anywhere with you—because Jesus knows that who you are at home is who and what you really are." As Zacchaeus and Jesus walked away with their arms around each other, I could hear Zacchaeus singing:

> *"Jesus saves to the utmost.*
> *He will pick you up, and he'll turn you around.*
> *Hallelujah . . . yes, Jesus saves."*

CHAPTER 9

THERE'LL BE SOME CHANGES MADE

Luke 19:1–10

Warren W. Wiersbe

My favorite version of *A Christmas Carol* by Charles Dickens stars George C. Scott as Ebenezer Scrooge. I like it best, because Scott portrays Scrooge the way Dickens wanted him portrayed, not as an inhuman miser or a selfish rogue but as a shrewd and successful businessman. Scrooge worked hard to get where he was, and he expected other people to do the same. He might have felt right at home with some of the men and women who run Fortune 500 companies today. Scrooge obeyed the law, but he forgot the two great commandments—to love God with all his heart and to love his neighbor as himself.

I think Zacchaeus was a lot like Scrooge. He did his work well and became very wealthy, but little by little he lost touch with the important things of life. Just as Scrooge became a new man in one short night, so Zacchaeus became a new man in one short day— the day he met Jesus. You can't come face to face with Jesus and stay the same. When Jesus looked up at Zacchaeus, he may have been thinking, "My friend, there'll be some changes made."

Let's consider some of these changes that occurred in the life of Zacchaeus, and let's try to learn what those changes mean to us today.

The first change was the beginning of all the rest: he started out an adult and ended up a child. The man became a boy. The people in Jericho knew the man Zacchaeus and didn't like what they knew. To them, he was a traitor to the nation of Israel because he was a Jew working for the Romans. That was bad enough, but he was also the manager of a staff of tax collectors, some of whom were more like extortioners. When the citizens of Jericho saw Zacchaeus coming, they gave him wide berth. They didn't want him for a friend.

But then things changed, and the man began acting like a child. He started running! That was strange, because back in that time and place, dignified men didn't run in public. Zacchaeus saw what looked like a parade coming down the street, and children love to watch parades. Like a child, Zacchaeus became curious. Why the crowd? Who was this man leading the crowd? He heard the name Jesus and decided he wanted to see this Jesus for himself. Not only did he run like a child, but like a child, he climbed a tree. Grown men, especially rich and powerful men, don't go around climbing trees, but little boys do. Zacchaeus started out an adult and ended up a child.

This fact reminds us of what Jesus had to say to the proud people of his day and of our day: "I tell you the truth, anyone who will not receive the kingdom of God like a little child will never enter it" (Luke 18:17). The world says, "Be a man! Be a woman!" And there are times when that's excellent counsel. But when it comes to becoming a citizen of God's kingdom and having your sins forgiven, the only counsel we need is, "Become like a child." Not childish, but childlike, willing to throw convention to the wind in order to get to Jesus.

Augustine said, "Shepherds and artisans oft enter the kingdom of heaven, while wise men and scholars are fumbling to find the latch." Peter wrote, "God opposes the proud but gives grace to the humble" (1 Peter 5:5). We're saved by God's grace, and you don't earn grace or deserve grace. You come to God like a little child and by faith receive grace as his gift. That was the first change Zacchaeus experienced as he moved toward meeting Jesus: he humbled himself, and the adult became a child. Have you done that? It takes humility to admit that we're sinners in need of a Savior. God still opposes the proud and gives his grace to the humble.

There was a second change in the life of Zacchaeus: he started out seeking and ended up being found. Jesus looked up to where Zacchaeus was perched in the tree, called him by name, and told him that he was going home with him. Why? Jesus told him why: "For the Son of Man came to seek and save that which was lost" (v. 10). Zacchaeus was seeking to see Jesus, but Jesus was seeking to find Zacchaeus—and a seeking Savior and a seeking sinner found each other!

When the people around them saw Jesus going home with Zacchaeus, they were shocked. "He has gone to be the guest of a 'sinner,'" they gasped. They were right; Zacchaeus was a sinner, but not for the reasons imagined by the people of Jericho. He wasn't a sinner because of his job or his wealth. He was a sinner for the same reason all of us are sinners: he was born in sin. Jesus didn't come to save the self-righteous and the religious crowd. He came to save sinners, and that includes you and me. Zacchaeus was born a Jew, a son of Abraham, but now he became a "child of Abraham" because he had been saved by faith. Paul wrote that "those who believe are children of Abraham" (Gal. 3:7). Abraham was saved by faith, because that's the only way anybody can be saved.

After Adam and Eve sinned, they ran away and tried to hide, but the Lord came to seek them. He found them and forgave them. When Jesus came to earth, he continued the Father's work and sought out the lost. Today, the Holy Spirit is seeking the lost through the witness of the church. Evangelist Billy Sunday said that sinners don't find the Lord for the same reason criminals don't find a policeman: they aren't looking! But Jesus is seeking for them just as he sought for Zacchaeus, and even if they aren't looking for Jesus, he's looking for them. There comes a time in life when the sinner meets the seeking Savior, and that's the time for the sinner to say to the Savior, "Lord, I believe!"

Let's look at a third change: Zacchaeus started out a poor man and became a rich man. No, that statement isn't reversed; it's correct. Zacchaeus *thought* he was a rich man, and so did his neighbors, but he was actually a poor man. He was rich in things material but bankrupt in things eternal. He was like the people in the city of Laodicea that Jesus described: "You say, 'I am rich; I have acquired wealth and do not need a thing.' But you do not realize that you are wretched, pitiful, poor, blind, and naked" (Rev. 3:17). Our Lord asked one day, "What good is it for a man to gain the whole world, yet forfeit his soul?" (Mark 8:36). How we answer that question determines where we spend eternity.

Certainly it's good to have the things that money can buy, provided we don't lose the things money can't buy. What good is it to own an expensive house if there's no loving home inside? What's the eternal benefit of owning the latest and most expensive automobile if you are driving down the broad road that leads to destruction? Jesus said, "What is highly valued among men is detestable in God's sight" (Luke 16:15), and that includes many of the luxuries that advertisers make us think are necessities.

Zacchaeus exchanged the temporary wealth of this world for the eternal wealth that can come only from Jesus. So thrilled was he with this newfound eternal treasure that he promised then and there to give half of his possessions to the poor! He had experienced the riches of God's grace, the grace that is greater than all our sins. He had received the riches of God's mercy. When you belong to Jesus Christ, the only bankbook that counts has but one entry in it: "And my God will meet all your needs according to his glorious riches in Christ Jesus" (Phil. 4:19).

When I was confirmed, our confirmation hymn was Harriet E. Buell's song "A Child of the King." The first stanza says,

> *My Father is rich in houses and lands,*
> *He holdeth the wealth of the world in His hands!*
> *Of rubies and diamonds, of silver and gold,*
> *His coffers are full, He has riches untold.*
> *I'm a child of the King, a child of the King!*
> *With Jesus my Savior, I'm a child of the King!*

Are you a child of the King? Do you have access into the treasury of God's grace and mercy? It's a great day in your life when you exchange the useless trinkets of this world for eternal wealth in Christ Jesus. Think of the price that Jesus paid to make this wealth available to us! "For you know the grace of our Lord Jesus Christ, that though he was rich, yet for your sakes he became poor, so that you through his poverty might become rich" (2 Cor. 8:9).

Zacchaeus started out an adult but became a child. He started out seeking and ended up being found. He started out poor and became rich. Let's consider another change: he started out small but ended up big.

Zacchaeus was a short man who couldn't see Jesus because of the crowd that lined the street. Nobody offered to lift him up, so he climbed up the nearest tree to get a better view of the man at the head of the parade. By what standard do you measure yourself or other people? Is it by physical standards? Basketball coaches value men for their height, while the air force rejects potential fliers who are too tall. Photographers look for models that are beautiful and handsome, but nobody worries about your looks if you're applying to earn a Ph.D. What we are physically comes from our genetic pool, and we can't take credit for it. God looks beyond all that and examines the heart.

All of us are like Zacchaeus in that we are all too short. "For all have sinned and fall short of the glory of God" (Rom. 3:23). All of us are too short to meet God's perfect standard of righteousness as revealed in Jesus Christ. Let's you and I go out to the beautiful state of Colorado. I'll go down into a coal mine, hundreds of feet below the surface of the earth, and you climb Pikes Peak. Both of us hear God say, "Touch the stars!" We stand on tiptoe, trying to touch the stars, and we can't reach them. We're too short. No matter how low or how high we may be in this world, we're still too short to meet God's holy standards. That's why we need to come to Jesus, because he specializes in making little people big by his grace.

Saul of Tarsus thought he was a big man with great authority, but Jesus knocked him off his horse, blinded him, and made him small enough to be saved. Saul would have lived and died just another religious man, but Jesus saved him and changed him. Saul became Paul, and in Latin, *paulus* means "small." Paul called himself "less than the least of all God's people" (Eph. 3:8) and "the worst of sinners" (1 Tim. 1:15). Like Zacchaeus, Paul saw and heard Jesus and trusted in him, and this made him a different person.

God is no respecter of persons. We don't impress him by who we are, what we do, or what we own. All of us are too short to touch the stars. But Jesus came down from heaven as a little baby; he made himself small that he might make us big—and when you put your faith in him, you experience the true greatness of being a child of the King. David said in Psalm 18, his victory psalm, "You stoop down to make me great" (v. 35). Jesus came down to our level and was made sin on the cross, that he might lift us up to his level to share with him the glory of his eternal throne. Hallelujah, what a Savior!

That leads us to another change: Zacchaeus started out guilty and ended up righteous. When Jesus started home with Zacchaeus, the people in the crowd criticized Jesus. They said, "He has gone to be the guest of a 'sinner'" (v. 7). The crowd was echoing the accusation the Pharisees often voiced, "This man welcomes sinners and eats with them" (Luke 15:2). Without realizing it, these critics were preaching the gospel. They saw Jesus as a sinner, and that's the way the Father saw Him when Jesus died for us on the cross. Jesus was "numbered with the transgressors" (Isa. 53:12; Luke 22:37) and treated like a guilty criminal. *We* were the guilty ones, but he willingly took our place. "He himself bore our sins in his body on the tree" (1 Peter 2:24).

The name Zacchaeus comes from a Hebrew word that means "pure." But Zacchaeus hadn't lived up to his name, nor can we claim to be pure, "for all have sinned and fall short of the glory of God" (Rom. 3:23). There's no question that Zacchaeus was the guilty one and Jesus was the pure one, but God in his grace reversed them. Jesus became the guilty one, and Zacchaeus received cleansing and forgiveness and the righteousness of God because he surrendered to the Savior. It was Jesus who took the blame and Zacchaeus who received the blessing.

We live today in a society that doesn't concern itself with personal guilt. The important thing is that you don't get caught, and even if you do get caught, there are many ways to get out of paying the fine. But there's coming a day when God is going to judge the world in righteousness, and on that day there will be no hiding behind legal technicalities or paying bribes. People who don't stand before God dressed in the righteousness of Jesus Christ will hear him say, "I never knew you. Away from me, you evildoers!" (Matt. 7:23).

The history of salvation is seen in trees. Our first parents disobeyed God and brought sin into this world. They hid from the Lord God among the trees of the garden. Zacchaeus climbed up a tree so he could see Jesus, but Jesus was nailed to a tree so he could save all who come to God through him. Jesus changes people. Jesus can change you. What a difference a day makes when that day is the day of your salvation!

CHAPTER 10

A CONVERSATION ABOUT
THESE SERMONS

Warren, you began your sermon by comparing Zacchaeus to Scrooge. How did you come up with this comparison, and what were you trying to do by using this analogy?

Wiersbe: Well, I was watching the George C. Scott version, and it just hit me that this man is doing Scrooge the way Dickens wanted it done. Scrooge was not some little wizened miser. He was a successful businessman, Fortune 500. So I thought that's a good way to start. Plus, nobody agrees with me, so they would listen. They'd say, "I'm going to prove this man wrong yet." So it was kind of a small shock to the listeners. But we started on common ground, and I thought that was a good way to do it. By the way, this is a new introduction to an old sermon.

You also bring out some of the cultural background of the original setting of the text. Why do you think that's important in a sermon?

Wiersbe: Well, our job as expositors is to build a bridge to an old book for people today. We're connecting the ancient with the modern, and people don't quite understand what a publican was. They think of a republican. So I thought we better get some of that in there. But E. K. did the same thing. He got that background in there too.

E.K., you began your sermon by inviting people to go with you on a journey. Is that an approach you've used in other messages? Is it something you use only in a narrative text? Do you also use this approach in a didactic text?

Bailey: Well, I think this approach is much better when preaching a narrative, because you are inviting the people to participate in the message with more than their minds, but also with their eyes, ears, and emotions. The message becomes very personal because the characters come alive, and it delivers the listener to the scene in a way that is very difficult to do with a didactic text—although one must be very creative in order to use that approach with a didactic text; it fits better in narratives.

Wiersbe: I think the didactic text really demands a lot of imagination. I know I did a sermon from Philippians 4 in which we started in the treasury, "My God shall supply all your need," then we moved someplace else, and moved someplace else. I was imposing an imaginative grid, and that wasn't good exegesis, but it did hold the sermon together.

Bailey: A lot of Old Testament texts are great narratives. When you preach them in a didactic way, it blends the best of both approaches. There are great stories in the New Testament. Most of the epistles are didactic; therefore, it requires much greater imagination to use the journey genre.

Wiersbe: You know, maybe going on a journey is a good metaphor for preaching in general. I mean, you start something, you know where you're starting, and you know where you're going. I don't know that we always know where we're going, but you've got those way stations along the way.

Bailey: If your points or your moves can be way stations, then you allow those way stations to be points of connection. As you travel from one way station to another, you are allowing the people to move along with you in the caravan, and if you can imaginatively describe those way stations, points, or moves, then I think the journey idea will be more effective.

Wiersbe: My problem, though, brethren, is that when I'm on this journey, I sometimes run out of gas!

One of the things I notice is that both of you make multiple references to songs and hymns and even quote the lyrics in your message. Is that fairly typical of your preaching? Why did you use lyrics with this particular sermon?

Wiersbe: Well, you actually sang, as I recall. You sang "Amazing Grace," didn't you?

Bailey: I sang about four songs; I did the unthinkable. The number of songs is very unusual, but not the actual singing. Periodically I will do that. It has a number of effects. Number one, it allows the congregation to breathe intellectually. If you're driving a standard shift, you don't want to keep the car in first gear all the time. So you must shift gears and give the congregation time to intellectually breathe and transition so they won't be in sustained and intense listening mode for thirty to forty minutes to an hour. It also brings in a cultural relevance. The singing occurred in the middle of the sermon. Wherever I've preached this sermon, all of the people were familiar with the songs; in fact, the people started singing along with me. However, if I were preaching this sermon to a white congregation, I probably wouldn't do as much singing, and if I did, I would alter the songs to be more relevant to that particular culture. Finally, it draws the listener in and makes the sermon much more participatory.

Wiersbe: I think emotion comes in there.

Bailey: Absolutely!

Wiersbe: Because music not only has words; it's also got melody, and every song reminds somebody of something. I remember when he preached this message. It really stirred us. I thought, "Well, we're getting twice as much for our money tonight."

Bailey: Wait a minute, Wiersbe, are you promoting emotion in the white church?

Wiersbe: Oh yeah. We're trying to defrost God's frozen assets in this sermon.

Bailey: But I think it's very important. I've always felt that emotion used properly is essential, because God not only made us cognitive, but he also made us emotive. In many of the white settings, we've ruled out emotions completely, and to do that takes away from our humanity and de-emotionalizes us to the point where we are stripped of any passion regarding what we are doing.

Wiersbe: Amen. The white brothers have saved all their emotion for the business meetings, not for the worship services.

Bailey: And the ball games.

Wiersbe: I quoted my confirmation hymn. Half the congregations you preach to don't even know what confirmation is. But I thought, "Here's a slice out of my young life and what that song meant to me, and maybe it'll get through to them."

E. K., Suppose you had preached this sermon in a seminary chapel somewhere, and the following hour the students gathered either in a homiletics class, or maybe better yet in a hermeneutics class, to discuss your sermon. What do you think the students and the professor might say?

Bailey: First, I think their responses would be based on whether they were right- or left-brained thinkers. Because the left-brained students would probably run me out of town on a rail and proclaim that I violated every homiletical principle known to man.

Wiersbe: *Almost* every.

Bailey: Yes, almost every. The right-brained would rejoice over the creativity, the excellence, with which I hope the sermon was communicated. Regardless of the approach, the risk was worth the reward of communicating that ultimately Jesus is the answer to the human condition, and it encourages people who find themselves in similar situations as did those four persons in the text. They found themselves facing blindness, long-standing sickness, demonic activity, and death.

Wiersbe: You know, I have played that tape to my seminary classes. It's one of the little things I do because we have to separate the left-brained from the right-brained. And every doctor of ministry class to which I've taught the Imagination Course has broken down to about 15 percent left-brained and 85 percent right-brained. The latter are really searching for beauty, for emotion, for imagination. Fifteen percent are lost someplace in I don't know what, and they didn't like the sermon. They'd say, "Wait a minute, wait a minute; Zacchaeus did not collect the taxes. He was the boss of the collectors." Well, that day he collected. But the other folks were taking copious notes. They were saying, "Ah-ha. Now I see why he's doing this." And we would discuss it. I was glad E. K. wasn't there. But most of them voted to give him an A+ on the message.

Let's turn the tables and ask this of you, Warren. What if you had the same experience, what do you think homiletics or hermeneutics students and professors might say if they had heard your sermon in a chapel?

Wiersbe: I think I would pass in hermeneutics and homiletics. But I would not pass in delivery, because it's a little bit too left-brained. It's a little bit too organized. Not that E. K.'s isn't organized; it is. But mine lacked that overriding metaphor. I should have developed more the idea of "There'll be some changes made." Now, there's a metaphor there that needed to be worked on, and I think if I'd have put a couple of more hours into praying, meditating, and imagining, I could have done a better job. But I'd probably pass in hermeneutics and homiletics, but—

Bailey: Now, why do you say that, Doc?

Wiersbe: On homiletics: it was an understandable sermon. And it was not just a bare outline. On hermeneutics: I think I exegeted the passage safely, but it lacked that cultural context that made the listeners participants. That was the biggest weakness of the message. So if I were to preach it down at Concord Baptist, I'd have to rework the whole thing. But any man who dares to preach on Zacchaeus down there is a fool.

Bailey: Now, Doc, I went back and read your sermon, and your sermon could be preached anywhere.

Wiersbe: Well, it needs better packaging. That's what it needs; it needs packaging.

Bailey: Yes, I agree that every sermon needs packaging.

Warren, before you introduce your fourth point in the sermon, you restate the first three points and then go to the fourth. So the outline is fairly clear to the listener. Is that important in today's audiences, and is that typical of your preaching?

Wiersbe: It's typical of my preaching, as my preaching is fundamentally teaching, but that is a dangerous thing because it calls too much attention to the outline and not enough to what the outline is saying. This is more of a left-brained sermon in that it is content-centered. And when you're dealing with content, you're dealing then with how this is put together. Whereas the way E. K.'s message is put together, you aren't lost; you know where you're going. But it's in the flow of context. So I felt at this point I'd better repeat what I'd said because some of them might have missed it.

Bailey: I kind of like that. Recapitulation, especially of the outline, keeps that bobsled in the middle of the track.

Wiersbe: You've been watching the Olympics!

Bailey: Yes, yes, I have. And it brings the listener back to the structure and the flow of the sermon. Now, you can overdo anything, but I think that as you move from one way station to another, it shows how you make the leap from one station to the next. When it's kept at a minimum, it especially adds the kind of proper elasticity that can connect one idea to the other.

Warren, you quote several authors in your sermon, and E. K., you don't include any quotes in this sermon. Why the difference? Does it have to do with the intended audience, or is it simply personal style differences?

Bailey: Well, I was telling a story as seen through the eyes of Zacchaeus; therefore, there wasn't a need to quote anyone else, because he was telling his own story. In the context of the personal testimony of Zacchaeus, it would almost be inappropriate to quote someone else's commentary on his life and his story—although in my normal teaching I would have many quotes from other people. However, when I preach narrative sermons, it would be awkward to stop and inject a quote in the midst of first- or third-person context.

Wiersbe: My sermon was preached at Moody Church. Consider the audience. You have everything there—students from Northwestern University, Moody Bible Institute students, people who wandered in from the street, maybe half drunk. I found that when I was at the Moody Church it was important to identify with different groups in the congregation. It's like preaching to the United Nations. We'd probably have forty different denominations represented and who knows how many nationalities. When preaching to this congregation, I didn't often quote people like Augustine. I might quote Wally Cox or Red Skelton, because the purpose of the quotation is to drive a nail in the wall.

E. K., you make use of some repeated refrains, and very effectively—for example, "Maybe I'll have better luck next time" or "Give me thirty days." Why did you use this tactic, and is it something you often use in your preaching? Is it characteristic of African-American preaching?

Bailey: I think it is. Earlier I mentioned the recapitulation idea and the repetition. Dr. King had a way of saying, "How long? Not long." That kind of recapitulation has been true to form in African-American preaching, and that's why I said earlier that I like it. It's not only a cultural thing; it's more than that. It refers back to what I mentioned earlier regarding the bobsled. It helps to facilitate the connectedness of the sermon, to build suspense, and to add a little humor, all of which I think are very important.

Wiersbe: I thought it was a brilliant thing to do, because it gives you a rhythm. There's a rhythm not only to the way the sermon is put together but to the way it's delivered. And it gave us a signal when you would say, "Well, maybe I'll have better luck next time," then we knew, uh-huh, we're going someplace else.

Bailey: We had disembarked, and it was time to reboard the train to move to the next location on our journey.

Wiersbe: And those signals are so important, so important.

E. K., what are some of the responses you've heard and seen when you preached this sermon?

Wiersbe: You should have been there during the sermon. Excuse me, E. K., for interrupting, but . . . I sat next to Stephen Olford when you were preaching that sermon. And now, Stephen Olford is homiletics par excellence, alliteration out of this world. He was absolutely floored. He was crying; he was laughing. He entered into the message with great blessing. We all did. But when the sermon was preached, the congregation responded beautifully.

Bailey: And that's what I call delivering the congregation to the scene. And then pulling them into the experience, where they are walking with you to the extent that they even taste the dust from the road. They feel the rocks beneath their feet as we walk the roads together. They see the unkempt grass and the little shanty that we passed by. They are seeing all of this, and they even see the color of it and when it changes colors. And so I think it's very important to understand that unlike some sermons that remain aloof, distant, and dead, the characters come alive, and they come alive in the preacher's life and in the lives of the listeners. Of course, I've heard some very good creative preaching; however, for some people that's not acceptable. But for most people, the creativity is what they talk about, and for others, the encouragement that they received as a result of listening to the message.

Wiersbe: Well, it made me rethink a lot of my preaching. And when I would play the tape for my students, I'd say, "What's your first response?" And the left-brainers would say, "Not the exegesis," and before long we were discussing Barth and Brunner and that kind of stuff. But the other folks were saying, "Well now, that got to my heart, but he broke some of the rules." And of course that gives me the opportunity to say, "Look, when the rules have broken you, then you can break the rules. But first the rules have got to break you."

Bailey: And I am convinced that too much of our preaching is aimed at the head. For so long we have been a head-oriented society. We always want to capture the intellect. And I think too many of our people walk out of the church with an informed head and a cold heart. A person is not motivated to do what the head has been informed of; therefore, preaching that does not touch the heart will seldom reach the hand of implementation. And so a lot of my preaching has started to shift and change to go for the heart. I want to inform the head along the way. I'm not disparaging intellect at all, because I know the head must be informed. But it's the heart that really captures the will, and if the will can't be bent, the chances are greater that behavior will be impacted.

Wiersbe: And I think that they're teaching us now that unless you reach the imagination, behavior is not changed. And that's where the heart comes in.

The purpose of the book is to look at preaching in black and white and what we can learn from each other. So let's discuss a related question. Warren, do you think that E. K.'s sermon would work with a Caucasian audience, and E. K., do you think Warren's sermon would work with an African-American audience?

Wiersbe: Well, I think both of us are smart enough to know you have to adapt to wherever you are. Yes, his sermon would work with a Caucasian audience. But he would be wise enough not to preach that to an assembly of Ph.D.'s— who might desperately need it, but it wouldn't get through to them.

Bailey: It wouldn't get through at all.

Wiersbe: Now, mine would really have to be changed up if I preached it at Concord. As I said, the basic outline is good. Everything is fine, but it needs life, it needs pictures, it needs imagination.

Bailey: And I would agree with that. And I know that, of course, you've preached at Concord many times, and you always make the necessary adjustment.

Wiersbe: You have to or—

Bailey: Bring it to life. Now, what I liked about preaching to the African-American audience is that somehow through it all we have retained the best of our historical culture by not vilifying emotion, but we live in two worlds. We are able to do both simultaneously, that is to say, we have the ability to both listen and say "Amen" concurrently. We have to live in the Eurocentric world as well as the African-American world. So while we have retained the best of our culture, of appreciating emotion without succumbing to emotionalism, we have also the training from the white world where we appreciate the substance, the intellect, the brain. In a broader sense, when our experiences or when those two worlds are wedded, the possibility exists for us to have heavenly harmony and ministerial melody, but only when both the black and the white notes are played together.

Wiersbe: Well, I think that it would do our Caucasian congregations good to hear this kind of a message every once in a while. Because we get elitist. When you pick up a history of preaching, its emphasis is primarily on the Caucasian preacher. And I've put together many anthologies of sermons, and it's primarily the Caucasian preacher. We have the attitude sometimes that we can't learn anything from these brothers and sisters, but we sure can.

Bailey: Most of us who have been to seminary in the African-American world have gone to white schools. So it's obvious what we have learned from the white community and the white world and the white pulpit. But it's not obvious what can be learned from the black preacher by the white preacher and the white church.

Wiersbe: But maybe that's one reason why Beeson Divinity School has Robert Smith on the faculty.

Bailey: Oh, I know.

Wiersbe: You put Robert Smith and Calvin Miller together, and you've got something volatile.

Bailey: Yes, you do. And they bring the best of both worlds together. Because Robert is a classic example of the synthesis that I just described.

What impact did you hope your sermon would have on listeners? What did you hope to accomplish with this sermon?

Bailey: Well, my hope was to communicate that Jesus is the answer to life's greatest challenges. Jesus rescues those who wrestle with inferiority and inadequacy, and he helps us to overcome or to triumph over the tragedies of long-standing sickness, as with the issue of blood, the demonic oppression, or even death, as highlighted in the sermon.

Wiersbe: Well, my goal was to let people know the greatness of Jesus and that it's never too late to change. Now, I dealt more with the steps that were involved in this change. And actually everybody didn't need the whole sermon. There were those who were too much adult and needed to be children. There were those who were too big and needed to be short. There were those who were too rich and needed to become poor. So it was sort of a scattershot thing: "Lord, somebody, someplace in this crowd, is going to need this." So that at the end there can be changes made in my life, but that first step is, Will I let God do it? I can see many ways of improving this message, but there it sits.

PART 3

WE LEARN TOGETHER

CHAPTER 11

CONVERSATION ABOUT LEARNING FROM OTHERS

Wiersbe: We probably should point out that there are dangers as well as blessings in reading sermons, one of the first being the temptation to plagiarize other people's material. Mark Twain said that Adam was the only man who when he said something, actually knew it was original.

Bailey: It's all been said before; we just package it in a different way. I don't read sermons to borrow but to get blessed. I may not like the preacher's style or even his theology, but I can get help if I open my heart to truth.

Wiersbe: In fact, there's value to reading the people we don't always agree with. They make us think. They may look at familiar ideas in a different way and open up new paths for us to explore.

Bailey: That's right, and they may force us to rethink some things we've taken for granted. But there's another value in reading sermons: we see how different preachers can take the same text and come up with a variety of themes and approaches. That encourages me, because God wants us to be ourselves and expound the Word as it filters through the grid of our own lives and experiences.

Wiersbe: I have the sermons in my library indexed so I can compare them. After I've read a sermon and let it bless my own heart, I like to examine it and see how the preacher put it together. How were the text and theme introduced? How were the aim and direction of the message stated? How did the preacher transition from one main point to the next? What were the personal applications? Was the conclusion a real clincher?

Bailey: That's important, but we also need to keep in mind that the preacher might have taken a different approach with a different text. It's good for us to read many messages from the same preacher and get better acquainted with his or her homiletical skills. But let me point out another danger: a sermon in print isn't the same as a sermon in the pulpit. We preach to be heard, not to be read, and it's hard to hear the voice from the page if you haven't heard the preacher in person.

Wiersbe: When I was ministering with the *Back to the Bible* broadcast, I often had to edit transcripts of my radio sermons for publication, and it was a tough job. How do you convey the tone of your voice or the urgency of the theme? Italics and exclamation points can't begin to do the job. The readers can't hear your voice; they can't see your face or your gestures. But there is one advantage to the printed sermon: if you didn't understand something, you can always go back and read it again.

Bailey: It's best that we prepare our own message first and then read what other preachers have done with the passage. We can often incorporate a new insight or find a good quotation. Of course, we always give credit when we use somebody else's material.

Wiersbe: Especially when it comes to personal illustrations. Illustrations from history or from the latest news reports belong to everybody, but personal illustrations belong to the person who had the experience.

Bailey: Here's another danger we must avoid, and that's feeling intimidated because we can't preach as well—as smoothly—as the preacher we're reading. We need to remember that the sermon we're reading has been edited and polished. Very few sermons are printed just the way the preacher preached them.

Wiersbe: I have in my file an edited proof of one of Spurgeon's sermons, and it is really marked up. By the way, radio sermons are also carefully edited.

Bailey: Preachers today have a rich treasury of sermonic material—books, cassette tapes, even videos—and it's a shame we don't make better use of it. But younger preachers have to beware lest they unintentionally start to imitate some favorite preacher, some pulpit giant they admire. God wants his messengers to be voices and not echoes.

Wiersbe: Acts 19:15—"Jesus I know, and Paul I know, but who are you?"

Bailey: You're a thief, that's what you are! And your conscience ought to bother you! There's no substitute for a biblical sermon from the heart of God through the heart of a preacher who loves his people. Anything less is like sending your wife a used anniversary card some other fellow already sent to his wife. You erase his name and sign your own, but that doesn't make it right.

CHAPTER 12

BIOGRAPHIES OF
BLACK PREACHERS

A rtists, writers, and musicians study the lives and works of other artists, writers, and musicians. They do it not to imitate but to be inspired and instructed by other creative people. So why shouldn't we preachers listen to other preachers, learn about their lives and methods, and read and study their published sermons? A wealth of material is available about the science and art of preaching, as well as a wealth of printed sermons, and wise is the preacher—beginner or veteran—who makes good use of it.

The easiest and best way to get a broad overview of preaching is to read through *Twenty Centuries of Great Preaching*, edited by Clyde F. Fant Jr. and William M. Pinson Jr. (Word, 1971). This thirteen-volume set of books is a gold mine for the serious preacher. You will be introduced to the best-known preachers in church history, beginning with Jesus and the apostles and ending with Dr. Martin Luther King Jr. Along with an analytical biography of the preachers and their ministries, the editors include several sermons from each preacher and a helpful bibliography to direct you in your further study. Everything in the set is carefully indexed in volume 13 to make it easy for you to locate a preacher, a sermon, a fact from homiletical history, or an illustration from a sermon. We can't recommend this set too highly.

A second suggestion is that you read *The Company of Preachers*, by David L. Larsen (Kregel, 1998). This is a rich compendium of biblical and biographical material that emphasizes "Preach the Word!"

Dr. Larsen has gathered information from many volumes and has carefully documented the material. The bibliographies alone are worth more than the price of the book. He includes sermon outlines, not complete messages, and discusses them briefly. You end up knowing both the preachers and their philosophies of preaching. Here are nearly nine hundred pages of essential information that we as preachers ought to digest.

A third helpful volume is *Living with the Giants*, by Warren W. Wiersbe (Baker, 1993). The book examines the lives and ministries of thirty-two "pulpit giants" and includes bibliographies of books by them and about them. *A Treasury of the World's Great Sermons* (Kregel, 1977) and *Sermons of the Century* (Baker, 2000), both edited by Wiersbe, contain both sermons and brief biographies.

The only black preachers included in *Twenty Centuries of Great Preaching* and *The Company of the Preachers* are John Jasper and Martin Luther King Jr. This shouldn't be interpreted as editorial prejudice but rather as the result of the lack of available materials. The absence of recording equipment and stenographic skill prevented the early black preachers from preserving their sermons, and if they did have the money and facilities to print them, who among their people had the money to buy them? This has robbed us of the sermons of many gifted black preachers. It's only in recent years that homileticians and historians have seen the importance of recovering this important but neglected aspect of black history.

All preachers ought to read the sections about Jasper and King and go on to read the books about them that are recommended. Note that more recent collections of King's sermons have been published, including *A Knock At Midnight* (Warner, 1998).

White preachers in particular will want to get acquainted with some contemporary black preachers and their preaching, and we offer here a suggested but not exhaustive list. We recognize that a number of other individuals could have been mentioned. We also want the reader to know that this is not necessarily an endorsement of any individuals included in the list.

Charles E. Booth (1947–) has been the senior pastor of Mount Olivet Baptist Church in Columbus, Ohio, since 1978. He is a graduate of Howard University, Eastern Baptist Theological Seminary, and United Theological Seminary and was granted an honorary doctor of divinity degree by Virginia Seminary. The recipient of many honors and awards, Dr. Booth has preached and taught at numerous colleges, universities, and seminaries, as well as at denominational and civic gatherings. In 1993 *Ebony* magazine included him on their Honor Roll of Great Preachers. Dr. Booth is a frequent contributor to *The African American Pulpit*, published by Judson Press. His book *Bridging the Breach: Evangelical Thought and Liberation in the African American Preaching Tradition* was published by Urban Ministries (2000). He has sermons in *The African American Pulpit Millennium Edition* (Judson, 2000), *No Other Help I Know: Sermons on Prayer and Spirituality* (Judson, 1996), and *Outstanding Black Sermons*, vol. 3 (Judson, 1982). Along with his pastoral ministry, Dr. Booth is also serving as professor of preaching at Trinity Lutheran Seminary in Columbus, Ohio.

Caesar Arthur Walter Clark Sr. (1914–) pastored churches in Louisiana and Tennessee before accepting the pastorate of the Good Street Missionary Baptist Church, Dallas, Texas, in 1950. He is recognized as a patriarch among pastors. Twice he has been featured by *Ebony* magazine among their Outstanding Black Preachers (1984, 1994), and in 1996 Governor George Bush gave him the Outstanding Texan award. Dr. Clark's congregation has been involved not only in worship, teaching, and evangelism but also in special ministries in the medical field and with people with mental and emotional needs. Their Social Service Center and Child Care Center give material and spiritual assistance to hundreds of people annually. His ministry of over half a century at the same church has won Dr. Clark the love and esteem not only of his own people but of believers everywhere. He is sought after as a mentor, evangelist, and preacher.

Anthony T. "Tony" Evans (1949–) serves as senior pastor of the Oak Cliff Bible Fellowship and is president of the Urban Alternative, both of which are in Dallas, Texas. He is a graduate of Carver Bible Institute (B.A.) and Dallas Theological Seminary (Th.M. and Th.D.). Through his conference ministry, his many books, and his *Urban Alternative* radio program, aired on over five hundred stations, Dr. Evans is very well known to believers of all races. Moody Press, Word, Crossway, Focus on the Family, and Thomas Nelson have published his books. He is an articulate preacher of the gospel, a defender of the faith, and a promoter of responsible citizenship, racial equality, and family stability, all in the Christian context.

E. V. Hill (1933–), pastor of Mount Zion Missionary Baptist Church, is a preacher and teacher for conventions, universities, colleges, seminaries, Bible conferences, local churches, and citywide revivals throughout the world. He has been honored by *Time* magazine as one of the seven most outstanding preachers of the United States. He is well known through television and radio ministry and is a member of the board of directors of World Impact, the National Coalition for Traditional Values, and the National Negro Republican Advisory Committee.

Major J. Jemison (1954–) has pastored the Saint John Missionary Baptist Church in Oklahoma City since 1988. He is a graduate of Bishop College (B.A.), Perkins School of Theology (Th.M.), and Midwest Baptist Theological Seminary (D.Min.). Dr. Jemison has held numerous offices in the Progressive National Baptist Convention and has served as an adjunct professor at the Oklahoma Baptist University.

William Augustus Jones Jr. (1934–) is the son and grandson of Baptist ministers. He is a graduate of the University of Kentucky and Crozier Theological Seminary and earned a doctorate from Colgate Rochester Divinity School. He has also studied at the University of Nigeria and the University of Ghana. Dr. Jones has pastored the Bethany Baptist Church in New York City since 1962 and is recognized as a strong pulpiteer and a leader in the struggle for human rights and economic justice. The *New York Daily News* called him "the dean of New York's great preachers." His ministry has taken him around the world, and he has preached at key conferences. He has served as a visiting professor at Colgate Rochester Divinity School, Wesley Theological Seminary, Princeton Theological Seminary, Union Theological Seminary, and United Theological Seminary. Dr. Jones has published numerous books on the black church in America as well as books of sermons.

A. Louis Patterson Jr. (1933–) has pastored the Mount Corinth Missionary Baptist Church in Houston, Texas, since January 1970 and is widely recognized as a gifted preacher and expositor of the Word. In 1991 Morehouse College inducted him into the prestigious Martin Luther King Jr. Board of Preachers, and he has been a frequent preacher at the National Baptist Convention. His church is involved in effective evangelism, prison ministry, assistance to students, and training of youth. Dr. Patterson has helped to mentor more than fifty men who are today successfully pastoring their own churches. He is in great demand as a lecturer on preaching and ministerial leadership.

Sandy Frederick Ray (1898–) has pastored the Cornerstone Baptist Church of Brooklyn, New York, since 1944 and has served as president of the Empire Missionary Baptist Church of New York for over twenty-five years. A native of Texas, he was educated at Arkansas Baptist College and Morehouse College. He served on the staff of Saint Luke Baptist Church in Chicago, working with Dr. L. K. Williams, and then pastored Shiloh Baptist Church in Columbus, Ohio. His ministry at Cornerstone Baptist Church has been widely recognized, and his preaching has helped multitudes of people face and solve the problems of life. He has held offices in the National Baptist Convention, has served as a trustee of Morehouse College, and has preached and lectured at numerous conferences and educational institutions, including Union Theological Seminary. He is widely recognized as an effective evangelist. His book of sermons is *Journeying through a Jungle*.

Robert Smith Jr. (1949–) has served since 1997 as professor of Christian preaching at the Beeson Divinity School of Samford University in Birmingham, Alabama. He received his master of divinity and doctor of philosophy degrees from the Southern Baptist Theological Seminary. Dr. Smith pastored two churches in Cincinnati, Ohio, and has been a featured preacher at numerous ministerial conferences and denominational conventions.He has served as a guest lecturer not only at his alma mater but also at the New Orleans Baptist Seminary and the Lutheran School of Theology in Chicago. Dr. Smith is widely recognized for his scholarship in the area of homiletics and African-American preaching and churches. He coedited, with Dr. Timothy George, *A Mighty Long Journey* (Broadman Holman, 2000) and has contributed to *Preparing for Christian Ministry, The Abingdon Preaching Manual,* and *The Minister's Manual.*

Gardner Taylor (1918–) is currently senior pastor emeritus of the Concord Baptist Church of Christ, Brooklyn, New York, where he served from 1948 to 1990. During his long ministry there, he saw more than nine thousand members added to the church family and led the congregation in the construction of a new church plant and the formation of the Concord Baptist Church Elementary School, the Concord Nursing Home, and the Concord Seniors Residence. Dr. Taylor and the church have been active in community ministries and civil rights programs, and he was the first African-American to serve as president of the New York City Council of Churches. Fifteen schools have granted him honorary degrees, including Colgate University, Howard University, Oberlin College, and Tuskegee University, and he presented the Lyman Beecher Lectures on Preaching at Yale in 1976. President William Clinton granted Dr. Taylor the Presidential Medal of Freedom in 2000. He has often preached at the Baptist World Alliance and has lectured on preaching at numerous seminaries. From 1959 to 1970, Dr. Taylor preached on the NBC programs *National Vespers Hour* and *The Art of Living,* and Judson Press has released these messages in five volumes. "The Essential Taylor" is a recording (CD and cassette) containing six of Taylor's messages, also released by Judson Press. His books include *The Scarlet Thread, Chariots Aflame,* and *We Have This Ministry,* and he has contributed articles and sermons to numerous journals and sermon anthologies. *Time* magazine called him "the dean of the nation's black preachers."

Melvin Von Wade Sr. (1944–) pastors the Mount Moriah Baptist Church on the border of downtown Los Angeles and has served the church and community there since 1975. His previous pastorates were the Bethlehem Baptist Church in Dallas, Texas, and Mount Pilgrim Baptist Church in Houston, Texas. He is a graduate of Bishop College in Dallas and did graduate work at Perkins Theological Seminary at Southern Methodist University. He is general secretary of the National Baptist Convention and has also been active in the work of the NAACP. He is coauthor with his brother and father of *These Three,* volumes 1 and 2.

Wyatt Tee Walker has been senior minister of the Canaan Baptist Church of Christ in the Harlem community of New York City since 1967. He received his B.S. and M.Div. degrees from Virginia Union University and his doctorate from the Rochester (New York) Theological Center. He has done postdoctoral studies at the University of Ife in Nigeria, the University of Ghana, and the Haitian-American Institute in Port-au-Prince. Dr. Walker is a recognized authority on African-American religious music and the African-American church, and he has published twenty-one books. He has been very active in civic and community affairs in Harlem, and his ministry of preaching and lecturing has taken him to nearly one hundred countries. The church sponsors nineteen outreach ministries to serve the people of Harlem. Dr. Walker has taught at New York Theological Seminary, United Theological Seminary in Dayton, Ohio, and Union Seminary in New York City. His books and videos are available from the Canaan Baptist Church of Christ: fax (212) 866–0720; phone (212) 866–0301.

Kenneth C. Ulmer (1947–) has been pastor of the Faithful Central Bible Church of Inglewood, California, since 1982. He is a graduate of the University of Illinois, with additional studies at Pepperdine University, Hebrew Union College, Oxford University, and the University of Judaism. He earned his doctorate at the Grace Graduate School of Theology, Long Beach, California. He has taught at Grace Theological Seminary, Fuller Seminary, Biola University, and Pepperdine University. In 1994 Dr. Ulmer was consecrated bishop of Christian education at the Full Gospel Baptist Church Fellowship, and in 2000 he was installed as presiding bishop over the Macedonia International Bible Fellowship, representing the nations of Zimbabwe, Namibia, England, the Republic of Congo, South Africa, and the United States. He has ministered widely as a preacher and lecturer.

Robert H. Wilson Sr. (1924–) is the founding pastor of Cornerstone Baptist Church of Christ in Dallas, Texas, organized in 1981. He earned his B.A. at Benedict College and his B.D. at Benedict School of Theology and holds three honorary degrees. He served churches in South Carolina and Florida before moving to Dallas to pastor the Saint John Baptist Church from 1966 to 1981. Active in the National Baptist Convention, he serves as director of the Congress of Christian Workers and as a member of the Board of Managers of the Foreign Mission Board. He is also president of the Dallas Baptist Ministers Conference. He organized the Bethlehem Foundation to serve the indigent population in Dallas, especially youth "ensnared in the criminal justice system."

Preachers wanting to get better acquainted with contemporary black preaching will want to subscribe to *The African American Pulpit*, a homiletical quarterly that publishes sermons by a variety of black preachers as well as articles relating to the African-American church. This journal is published by the Judson Press, PO Box 851, Valley Forge, PA 19482-9897. Judson Press has also published numerous books of sermons by black preachers, as well as studies of black preaching and the black church in America. You may write them for a catalog.

In 1981 Baker Book House published three excellent books by J. Solomon Benn III on black preaching, including specimen sermons:—*Preaching in Ebony, God's Soul Medicine,* and *Preaching from the Bible.* You may find copies in a used-book store. They are worth searching for. Another relevant book is *King Came Preaching: The Pulpit Power of Martin Luther King Jr.* by Mervyn A. Warren, published by InterVarsity Press. This book looks at King's sermons through the lens of current speech and communication theories.

Black preachers not yet acquainted with the sermons available from white pastors should consult the bibliographies in the books mentioned at the beginning of this chapter. The sermon anthologies offer the best opportunity for reading and studying their sermons. The messages of Charles Haddon Spurgeon, G. Campbell Morgan, D. Martyn Lloyd-Jones, John Henry Jowett, F. B. Meyer, F. W. Robertson, and George W. Truett have been staples of the minister's diet for years. A visit to any good bookstore that carries religious books will let you know who today's preachers are and what they have published.

Contemporary white preachers might be categorized into those who are homileticians who have written and taught preaching and those who are practitioners known for their pulpit ministry, often accompanied by a media ministry. We offer here a short list that is not exhaustive but merely representative. Biographical information as well as samples of sermons can often be found by doing an Internet search by name. This is especially true of those preachers who have a media ministry.

Homileticians:	*Practitioners:*
Elizabeth Achtemeier	William Franklin Graham
Bryan Chapell	R. Kent Hughes
Fred Craddock	David Jeremiah
Calvin Miller	John MacArthur
Stephen Olford	John Piper
Haddon Robinson	John R. W. Stott
	Charles R. Swindoll

We want to hear from you. Please send your comments about this book to us in care of the address below. Thank you.

GRAND RAPIDS, MICHIGAN 49530 USA

WWW.ZONDERVAN.COM

For further information about E. K. Bailey
and his conferences on expository preaching,
visit the following web site:
http://www.ekbailey.org/